What Others are Saying

Barb has written a heartfelt and practical book. She eloquently makes the connection between biblical truth and everyday life. She beautifully addresses the question: "How should I then live?" This is really the reason we seek truth. Her book adds texture to our basic existential faith questions with analogies that are deep and meaningful.

George Kenworthy, PhD, EdD
Missionary

Too many people in the evangelical community have given up on there ever being revival in our nation and in the hearts of today's young adults. Barb Yo (Ylitalo) has reminded us that God is still ready to fight for and with us who believe on His name. She inspires us to believe that He can change a generation and our nation. Thank you, Barb, for sounding aloud this important truth that God is not dead—He is alive and well!

D. James Johnson
Missions Pastor, Rocky Mountain Calvary Church, Colorado Springs, Colorado

Barb wrote a book so powerful and different. I love how she mixes truth with real-life examples of people living it out.

Camryn Wentzel
Student at Colorado Christian University

This should be required reading for college students; it was such a fresh word for today. I am so inspired!

Allison Fries
Student at University of Wisconsin Eau Claire

This book has not only given me examples of what living life as a warrior for Christ looks like, it has equipped me to *become* a strong warrior for Christ.

Anthony Clarke
Student at St. John's University, Minnesota

THE TIME TO TESTIFY

Let's Revive the Campus

Mary—
God has so much
for you ♡
— BARB

Barb Vo (Vlitalo)

Dedicated to:

Jesus—my King

Mark—my love

Jack, Brooke, Ryan, Bradley,

Abby, Katie, and Jasmine—my heart

And to the many young adults

I worship with—may you be inspired.

Micah 6:8

Acknowledgments

Thank you, Jesus, we did it! I pray I have revealed Your heart and honored this call to make warriors for Your kingdom.

I could not have accomplished this call on my heart without the support of you, Mark. Thank you for the encouragement to continue and for your blessing.

Thank you, Jack, Brooke, Ryan, Brad, Abby, and Katie. What a privilege it is to be your Mom. Thanks for your interest and help in this great task. You have taught me so much and continue to amaze me. I love you more than you can imagine.

To the many I mentor, and you know who you are, thank you. The privilege you give me to hear your heart, and walk with you rocks my world and challenges me in the best of ways.

Thanks to my mom and dad, who will always be my biggest fans. I miss you every day Papa.

Thanks also to the Bromstad family that demonstrated a walk with Jesus that intrigued me, and inspired me to surrender to His good plans, especially to you, Dyonne.

I will always be grateful, Grant, that you allowed me to serve in your ministry. It gave me a place to grow and to heal.

Thanks to Peter, Tim, Mitch, Zach, Michael, Carl, Kristin, Noah, Kalie, Kojo, Heidi, Nate, Andrew, and Engels for serving alongside of me. All of your hearts for Jesus are knit into these chapters in some way.

Thank you to my original editors Jil, Dan, Emily, Brooke, Ryan, and George Kenworthy. Your honesty propelled me forward.

Thanks also to Laurel Bunker. God used you to validate this message, and you gave me the energy for my final miles. Thank you also for writing the foreward. It is such a gift to partner with you.

Thank you to author Andy Andrews for your much needed advice and support on this book.

Thanks to 5 Fold Media for your professional coaching service. You are now family to me.

Thank you, Cathy Sanders, for overseeing this manuscript project. It is amazing to have publishers who loves Jesus—your input was invaluable.

Thanks to Alex Rybarczyk, Julie Rybarczyk, Abby Ylitalo and Emily Haataja, for using your gifts of marketing, graphic arts, and design and for being you, beautiful you.

Thank you to all of you who wrote a devotional for this book, I am forever grateful. Nate, Noah, Brooke, Allison J, Allison F, Jenna, Connor, Olivia, Ryan, Anthony, Charlie, Jessie, Lauren, Cash, Andrea, and Sarah. What a blessing you are, each of you are so gifted.

Thanks also to the family of Herb Brooks for allowing me to use his inspirational story, the Fritz family, the Shalom Birthing Center, and the family of Jordan Davis. Each of you inspire so many.

I wish I could write the names of each of you that I mentored, for I thought of you constantly as I wrote, along with my children, nieces, and nephews. I love you fiercely, and I pray this life lends us much more time to bond. Always remember Jesus is on your side.

Contents

Foreword

For over twenty-five years I have found myself captivated by the group of individuals that we call millennials, teens, or young adults. They are by far my favorite group to laugh with, to cry with, to dream with, and to cherish. I cannot say what began this love affair with a particular group that many finds difficult to understand and to relate to. Perhaps it was my first volunteer experience with our church youth group, when I—barely an adult myself—began to work with a scraggly group of high schoolers who had a distain for church and an even greater angst regarding adults, rules, and instructions as to how to dress, speak, walk, or behave. Some of their feelings were legitimate. More than anything, kids desire to be loved and accepted, not lectured to or spoken about. By and large youth are more than aware of their "oddities" and inconsistencies. They feel the pain of their changing bodies, acne covered skin, popularity problems, and hormonal peaks and valleys. They feel the sting of loneliness, the hunger of longing and love, the want to be pretty or handsome, and the woes of being misunderstood. For some of us this is part of what makes working with them so desirable. They are fragile yet strong, needy yet independent, filled with biting sarcasm, yet brimming with hope, know-it-alls yet full of questions. The ministry that I worked with then was no exception.

In that first ministry assignment, several of our ministry's youth came from very difficult homes where they were raised by grandparents in lieu of absentee fathers and mothers. As loving as these grannies were, they could not always relate to the young ones they were raising. Some of the youth were blessed with great parents who offered them great stability, wonderful education, and one too many electronic toys which distracted them from learning deeper life lessons. Others lived with older siblings, an aunt or an uncle, or in the worst cases, they raised themselves, leaving from and returning to a solitary dwelling. Some of the challenges that youth faced stemmed from generational communication gaps, broken dress codes, and differing worship styles. The youth battled to speak the same "church" language that the elders spoke without stepping on toes or breaking sacred, unspoken rules—when they did, the corrections could come swift and sharp and without gentle regard. Though I did not share in their frustrations regarding adult leadership and interaction, I did understand their desperate need to be accepted and understood. Isn't that what we all desire, a place to be seen, known and desired in the most sacred way? Yes, I had known in my own teen years the absence of belonging, and because of this, my heart has always been drawn to these souls who seek to know and be known. What better, healthier way to do this than to introduce them to the One who sought to redeem us and make us His very own—Jesus Christ.

Barb Yitalo shares a similar heart and passion. Perhaps that is why we became instantly bonded as the result of a random chance meeting, working in the same University but in very different roles. A boundless ball of energy and enthusiasm for generation X, Y, Z, or any other category of young people, Barb knows the anguish of a rule-laden religious life which bars the soul and spirit from enjoying freedom in Christ. As a result, it has been her life's passion as a mother, a mentor, a minister, and a friend to steer young souls in a direction which brings clarity of focus, joy, and peace even in the midst of stormy inner or outer lives. On more than one occasion, I have known Barb to travel for miles to connect with a former student now out navigating the college or work world, simply to ensure that he or she knows that they are loved by God and by her. Sometimes these journeys are more like rescue missions, drawing a young person back to God through loving, challenging conversation as Barb knows from years of relationship when one is walking on a tenuous tight rope of a path that is leading nowhere, quickly. She lives and loves the Word of God, and because of

Foreword

that, she walks it out, showing young people that it is possible to love God, not because one has to, but because He first loved us—because surrendering to Him is worth the risk.

This book will be a blessing to all who read it. There is zero fluff, lots of love, and a healthy dose of challenge in every page. I read a fair amount of books that are written about millennials, but I believe this one is written to them, for them, in honor of them, and because we need them. So read on, whether you are a youth pastor, a parent, a mentor, or a friend. Read in hope, and read with a pencil and paper at your side. As you do, you will find yourself with questions as to how you may go deeper with the young ones in your life to challenge them to be more than they thought they could be. I personally will have several copies on my desk or in the trunk of my car to share with a bewildered young person in need of restoration or with those who seek to love and serve them better. Either way, God will speak and will move through Barb Yitalo's writing. Be encouraged.

Laurel M. Bunker
Dean of Campus Ministries and Campus Pastor
Bethel University

Introduction

My son Ryan is one of the 3.3 million high school graduates this year across our great nation. I am overwhelmed when I see this next season of his life taking shape. As a mother, mentor to many young adults, and employee at Bethel University, I find myself looking at this next stage with anticipation. I believe that this decade of youth across America are the most gifted young people in history. The Bible tells us that God pours out His Spirit on the young, the child-like, the humble, and the wanting. These are the qualities I have witnessed in this generation over the last decade and continue to be inspired by. The youth today give me hope for the future of our world, America, and the body of Christ.

Three years ago I felt a call on my heart to write to this generation as they go off to college. After writing for some time about what was on *my* heart for them, I heard God ask me to write what is on *His* heart for them. God shook my spirit and asked me to "make selfless warriors" for His kingdom. I was overwhelmed, but quickly realized this is ultimately His job to work out and that I am not alone. I know our nation needs change, and more of Jesus is the answer. Could now be the time? It is time to testify to our Great King, battle, and push back the enemy that is wreaking havoc on our culture.

In the process of writing, God began to show me specific areas that we needed to grow in spiritually so we could all be strong for battle. Like any good warrior needs food for their physical body, we need food for our spiritual body. It is our spiritual body that needs to work out

15

and build muscle to become effective warriors. As it came together, this book became a spiritual boot camp for the young Christian army.

As I was writing, God used the Word and its amazing truths to inspire me. At times, the process made it hard to sleep or even relate to the real world. I was overtaken by the task. Miraculously, it seemed that whatever chapter I was on, truth for what I was writing would come from every place I sought it. But the most amazing wisdom came from the very people I was writing to. I was amazed countless times when I heard of their faith and the lessons they learned and realized that the timing of their stories matched my chapter. This couldn't be coincidence! It became very apparent that Jesus wanted me to include these testimonies in my book, as they lend just as much truth and wisdom as any story in the Bible. God is the same yesterday, today, and always! Our very lives give great testimony to His mercy and grace, and strengthen the body of Christ.

Thankfully, we do not serve an absent God, but a God that desires to invest in our lives and live through us. He has not given up on our nation, nor will He quit fighting for us. Nothing illustrates His love better than our own testimonies. So at the end of each muscle-building chapter you will find testimonies from students whom I am blessed to know.

I pray that you are encouraged by my efforts in this book, and as always, may God receive all the glory.

Chapter 1: For Such a Time as This—Finding Courage

"Mordecai sent this reply to Esther: "Don't think for a moment that because you're in the palace you will escape when all other Jews are killed. ¹⁴ If you keep quiet at a time like this, deliverance and relief for the Jews will arise from some other place, but you and your relatives will die. Who knows if perhaps you were made queen for just such a time as this?" (Esther 4:13-14 NLT).

C ollege life gives each of us a huge circle of influence and the ability to walk, dine, and share life with hundreds of people. There is no other stage in our lives that allows us such influence. The growth we can have in Christ, His body, and the world around us is endless. Every gift, every lesson learned, every experience we have had with God so far will be used, tested, and poured out on this platform. If we have ever wondered when God is going to use us and with whom, the time is now and the people you are to testify to are within the hallways and classrooms on your campus.

America has done so much good, but the ugly truth is we have forgotten our roots. Our country is the only country in the present day that completely committed its land and future to God. The generations

> **The time is now and the people you are to testify to are within the hallways and classrooms on your campus.**

before us met in groups across our land and prayed continually for God's blessings. Like the Israelites of the Old Testament we have forgotten our roots and laid God aside. We have removed Him from the throne over America and replaced Him with idols.

The Israelites had two main gods they replaced the true God with. One was Baal, which was basically a god of money and power, and the second was Asherah, who was a goddess of sex and promise. If we think about it, money, power, and sex seem more like the gods of our country today than any other idol. It is true that there is nothing new under the sun.

During this time in Israel's history, the people were rampantly disobeying God. They had forgotten the laws of Moses, and decided they could control their own destinies. They celebrated and worshipped foreign gods and allowed the cultures of other kingdoms to shape their laws and festivities. This was not a fast change, but a slow transformation from honoring God's truth to holding high the reasoning of common men. Thankfully, God sent a king with a pure heart to lead them. In 2 Kings 22 we find the story of King Josiah, who started his reign at the age of eight years old. His father before him had littered the culture with idolatry and immorality of all kinds. Josiah, however, walked right with God, and after realizing the full extent of Israel's disobedience, he tore his clothes and repented before the Lord on behalf of the sin of all Israel. He prayed for mercy, knowing that God's judgment was sure to come for their sins. Josiah's first action after repenting was to turn his kingdom back to God. He stripped the land of idols, honored God's ways from the throne, celebrated the festivals that God's people had forgotten, and brought worship back to the temple. If we take time to model after Josiah's action's at this time in our own history, and take seriously our nation's plight, we will be ready for whatever comes our way.

As the body of Christ, we have not represented Jesus for who He is—we have not modeled a passionate walk with Christ nor a hunger for the Word. And this is just the start of what we have not accomplished, as we have fallen asleep in battle. I'm not speaking for everyone, and truly many of you come from homes where you were raised far from this judgment being described. But this complacency extends far beyond our homes and into our communities, schools, government offices, and even churches. We have not shown the boldness we needed to, but, as though we were sleepwalking, have allowed the enemy to walk brazenly into almost every facet of our culture. He is easily moving about and we have laid our weapons down as a body, and resigned ourselves to sit and watch the destruction.

There is now an urgent call to all of us to live boldly and walk in truth. We cannot afford to wait any longer. Jesus is calling us *all* to testify and shake our nation from the ground up. What does it mean to testify? Testify is a word we most often use when we are a witness in court, when there would be a reason why our voice needs to be heard. When we testify, we give light to the truth, bring evidence, and give a better picture for the jury or judge to make decisions. Ever since Jesus came to earth He has been on trial. Many have testified regarding Jesus and effectively raised Him up, but some have ruined His reputation. Colorful words and intellectual reasoning can often win over a jury, but when we speak of our King in a way that the world can tell that we know Him, it will give them pause.

I guess this call to the church today does not seem fair; past generations lacked boldness too, so it has not even been modeled well for us all. But we have the Holy Spirit, and living out our walk with Christ is the best choice we could make. Where we are small, He is strong. He would never ask us to do something that can be completed by our own power alone; if He asks us to step out, He expects us to lean on Him for the strength and ability that we lack to complete the task, and He will give us reinforcements like we could never fathom. If we want to experience God more fully, we need to answer His call one small step after the next. Sticking our neck out where it is scary—with prayer and humility—is the very best way to experience God and build our spiritual muscles.

By all of us giving God our gifts, we can become part of a revival to our land that inspires the world and disrupts the plans of the enemy.

THE TIME TO TESTIFY

Revival can allow the Eternal God to reign again across the pulpits of our churches, the courts of our nation, the podiums of our Universities, and every home in our community. All across America there are pockets of people who are crying out for His guidance and repair.

This could seem overwhelming, but this is ultimately God's work. We are vessels that are used best when we join Him by using our gifts and talents for the kingdom. We don't individually need to save the world, but we are called to join God in His pursuit of redemption for all. We know His love can break the chains of despair in our life and mold us into an unmovable warrior. Raising Jesus higher each day will change the atmosphere and provide breakthrough for the next generation to enjoy.

So how do we get ready for this battle? It would be great to have lots of time to prepare, but the truth is that we are already in the battle. Are we going to lie there and take bullets, or are we going to stand up and fight back? The enemy has our back against the wall and his hands around our throat. We need to cry out to Jesus like never before, and recognize that being complacent not only wounds the body of Christ, but also grieves the Holy Spirit.

The time to testify is now. Let's be a voice in the darkness. Let's be a menace to Satan that drives his army back. Together, we can shake the gates of hell and set the captives free. Let's

The time to testify is now. Let's be a voice in the darkness.

make so much noise for Jesus that our nation has to stop and notice, and kneel again to the Most High God. This happens when we reach out to those around us and show love to the lonely and lost. It happens by each of us focusing on what God wants from us, and being brave enough to answer His call.

When I think of someone who was greatly used in a season of her life that is similar to ours in America, it is Esther. In Esther's time, God's people had their backs against the wall and their future hanging by a shred. Sound familiar? Let's see what happens.

Esther

Esther was born in 492 BC, and she lived in Persia as a Jewish exile. She was an orphan being raised by her cousin Mordecai. Her king at the time reigned over the land from India to Ethiopia, his name was King Ahasuerus. He had such a large kingdom it was divided into 127 provinces, and was the greatest empire in the world at the time. He had wealth we can hardly imagine. At one point, he decided to have a feast for every official through his land in honor of himself, the feast lasted 180 days. After this, he hosted a seven-day feast for every citizen, rich and poor. Near the end of the seven-day feast he sent word to his wife, Queen Vashti, to come present herself before his guests. They were quite a drunken crowd at this point, so she refused.

This caused a great dilemma for the king. He loved Queen Vashti, but her defiance could make him appear weak to his enemies, and even to his own people. To save face, the king decided to divorce and banish his wife, and a search went out for a new queen. The most beautiful virgins in the land were sought out and collected for a "contest."

Esther was fourteen years old at the time, which was a common age for marriage. I can imagine that she had been taught that a Jew should never marry a non-Jew, and she grew up believing that she would never live separate from her home and community. But Esther was chosen by the search committee and brought to the palace. To refuse a king's decree would have cost Esther her life, so she had no choice but to be obedient. Esther was placed in the harem with the rest of the contestants and they had to be prepared for a full year with beauty treatments, lessons in etiquette, and official requirements before they were allowed to meet the king. Once they had sex with the king they were considered part of his harem. Even if he never called for them again they were considered his property, and could not leave the palace or seek a husband. Any dream of Esther's to be part of a proper Jewish family was over the day she was chosen for the king.

If you read on in the book of Esther, you find out that she kept her Jewish identity a secret as requested by Mordecai. This could not have been easy. Not only could she not tell anyone she was Jew, she also had to live like a Persian. She had to forego the dietary restrictions of a Jewess, and even the name *Esther* is believed to have been given to her when she arrived in the Harem, as her birth name was actually Hadassah. We can only imagine how lonely she must have felt.

Mordecai was a gatekeeper at the palace, and stayed close by to support Esther. However, nobody could find out that they were related, because Mordecai was a known Jew. Jews were hated by many in the palace and Mordecai worried about Esther's safety if their relation was discovered.

Because God placed favor on Esther and she rightly used her gifts, King Ahasuerus chose her to be the next queen. Shortly after she was chosen, the king asked a man named Haman to be his second in command. Haman went out to the gate one day and commanded people bow down to him, but Mordecai refused. So Haman devised a scheme that would cause the king to order all Jews in every province to be put to death. He told the king that the Jewish people denied his lordship and worshipped their own God. Haman's ancestors had been in a long battle with the Jewish people, and he secretly wanted them abolished. Mordecai's refusal to bow down to him created the avenue for Haman's vengeance to be played out.

After hearing of the new decree to kill the Jews, Mordecai asked Esther to do what she could to save her people. For Esther, this was a huge risk because she did not know if the king would call for her in time to stop the killings. Her only choice was to approach his throne without an appointment. She knew that many were murdered mercilessly for arriving unannounced in the king's chamber because it was assumed they were coming with murderous intentions. Esther reminded Mordecai that she will be risking her life to approach the king in his court, but in her spirit she knew she must try her best to save her people. At this point, Mordecai tells her that maybe, just maybe, she was born for such a time as this.

I love her first act in preparation for this moment. She tells Mordecai to get a message to every Jew, telling them to fast and pray for three days, saying that her maids and servants would do the

> **Esther was calling on heaven's power in do-or-die fashion.**

same. Esther was calling on heaven's power in do-or-die fashion. What wisdom she had! She told Mordecai basically, "If I die, I die." She knew that God was in charge, and understood that at this crossroad there was only one way for her to turn.

Obedience was one of her strong suits. In the end, because of her tact and craftiness, the king reversed his decree and killed Haman instead. The Jews were spared, and the story ultimately declares God's sovereignty. People prayed, Esther showed courage, and the true King handled it. It is always by His power that we defeat the enemy.

The Almighty God knit gifts and tools into Esther those first fourteen years, and He raised Esther up so He could use her position on the most powerful throne in the known world to complete His cause. As she left her home for the unknown world in the palace, she would never have dreamed her life would be used to save her family's lives, and the nation of Israel.

Every gift that God gave to Esther, every experience with God up to that point, every lesson she learned from Mordecai, and every prayer answered in her life was poured out at the moment she decided to do God's will. Esther was probably not secure in her earthly surroundings and relationships in the palace, but she was secure in God. She knew God was her constant. God could have saved the Jewish nation without Esther, but she heard His call, and decided to answer it.

What about our nation today? Are we ready to answer the call? We will not all be asked to be an Esther. We may be a Mordecai, a prayer warrior behind the scenes. But, if we all find our place and serve, we will see revival in America. It's not fun to stick our neck out, but it is imperative for us to try. Sitting around has gotten us nowhere. It is not a coincidence that in all of history we are on earth together right now, as one body, each of us a unique part of God's redemptive plan.

> **God could have saved the Jewish nation without Esther, but she heard His call, and decided to answer it.**

In 2 Corinthians 5:20, the apostle Paul tells us what our calling is as believers. He says that we are ambassadors to Christ, as though He were making an appeal through us. What does that really mean?

Being an ambassador in Jesus time has the same meaning as today's culture, but let's reflect on it a bit. If our president wanted one of us to be an ambassador to another nation, that would be intimidating. We would need some major briefing and time spent in Washington to get ready. It was the same in biblical days, but even harder. To be an ambassador you were responsible for knowing the heart and mind of the king in a very intimate way. Without modern technology, the ambassador was often sent to evoke the word of the king to other provinces and nations. They were relied on for knowing the king's opinion concerning many different current events.

To be a worthy ambassador they would have to spend a great deal of time with the king to intimately know his decision process and to represent him well. They would even have to relay the exact tone of a message that the king would speak. To be a good ambassador, both today and in the past, takes a very close relationship with your command. For us to do this well we need to know our Father's desires and His heart for everyone around us.

We already are God's ambassadors. If we misrepresent His heart we can do great damage to how He is perceived. Let's take this seriously because this world needs God's perspective and love more than ever before. People around us deserve a good and complete picture of who He is. This could change everything.

As it stands, we can find unrest in most every area of our culture. The body of Christ has been fighting among themselves, and the time has come for unity. Many in my generation fear

Your generation and mine together have everything we need to help repair our nation's opinion of Jesus.

the future condition of the church in America. But I believe that your generation and mine together have everything we need to help repair our nation's opinion of Jesus—bringing the peace only God can provide.

We will all have Esther moments, big and small. As we are all being prepared, knit, and empowered to be part of a mighty act of God. God has a call on our lives that we should not miss. We will never regret walking in obedience, pursuing His heart, and allowing Him to shape us through this important time.

What if all of us would give our next season to God, and ask Him to do with it what He wants? What if we used our gifts to the fullest to impact dorm floors, classrooms, and communities around us? What if a million young adults felt inspired to make this generation the most God-centered one of all? This inspires me, because I believe it is possible. God is waiting with miracles at the ready, and hearts that are prepared for harvest. God is saying, "Make ready the warriors, revival is coming."

The following chapters will walk through some key areas that can give us the spiritual muscles needed for this task, helping us to be the salt this world desperately needs. There is a Nazarene, a powerful Savior that can join us and help us become warriors for His kingdom step by step. God knows His will for us; it is our job to pursue Him and be ever ready "for such a time as this" in our own lives.

THE TIME TO TESTIFY

Meet Noah Grothe
Junior at Gustavus University
St. Peter, Minnesota

I have not met anyone more committed to learning about Jesus than Noah. I met him at camp last year in Montana and he has agreed to let me share his story. When Noah was just fifteen he came home from school and found that his father had tragically taken his own life. Noah was there with his mom and little sister, Grace, and a large crowd that came to his home to help them.

At one point, Noah went to his room to get away from the commotion and he turned his heart to God. This is how he described this important time: "When I got to my room I turned my heart to God and there was an incredible peace in the midst of everything. I told God that I knew this was not His fault, and that I knew He would take care of my family. All of this felt like a miracle of God's grace. From that day on His mercy has allowed me to keep seeking Him faithfully. He is still teaching me a lot about sonship and communing with Him. God positioned my heart toward Him early on and I have been looking to Him for fathering since that time."

God told Noah that He would be His father, and Noah said he would be His son. I find this miraculous that at this point he could hear God, and feel His presence enough to find peace. Noah then began to draw nearer and nearer to God. He began counting on God for counsel and direction in a real personal way. God not only revealed to Noah much about who he is, but mostly about who God is. As Noah passionately pursued God he became ever more vigilant about following His ways.

Noah is now a junior in college and a true example of God's work on his heart. Noah has an ear to God like I have never witnessed. He is obedient, discerning, humble, and has an incredibly peaceful presence. Noah credits God for this, but I feel Noah also deserves some credit. His ability to tune out the circus around him and hear God's voice does not happen without effort.

When we were at camp this last summer in Montana we were committed to spending time with our king. Many of my girls were spending quality time reading and studying their Bible, journaling, and listening for the voice of God. All the kids at camp were waiting on God with anticipation, knowing God is always near. One night I was barely finished hearing one story about deliverance or healing, when another person would run up to tell me what God did for them. It was wonderful!

There were countless times that Noah got a message from God for one of our campers, and it was very obvious that it was God sent. He did not know many of these campers, but God used Noah to provide an intimate, timely message for their spirits. When I told him this, he seemed embarrassed and never wanted people to credit him, as he was just being obedient to His Father.

Noah, like Esther, used all the knowledge He had received from God to bless so many. His pursuit of God and His ways brought fruit in abundance to our little group. I am grateful to God for revealing himself to Noah so we can see more of who He is. I aspire to hear God like Noah does. His dedication to drawing near to God has given him a powerful witness and a platform that blesses everyone around him, ultimately pointing us all to Jesus.

Meet Charlie Schmid
Youth With A Mission Leader
Kansas City, MO

Before I encountered God, I was trying so hard to believe my identity as His son. Somehow I believed that I needed to keep trying and performing to truly be His. Because of this misconception I stopped growing in my spiritual life. I was focused on myself and trying to do better instead of focusing on God. There are so many followers of Jesus who have that same mindset. We become so engrossed in ourselves and our performance that we actually forget to live out who we are. There was a lack of identity in my life. Once I truly encountered Christ I began to understand His ways. It was then that I realized that I am already His son because of what Jesus had done for me. I didn't have to do anything to earn that.

Then God showed me that it is from this place of knowing our true identity as sons and daughters of God that we actually can go and take ground for Jesus. God spoke over me and told me that I was His warrior. This new identity drastically changed my life from one of passivity and fear to one of power and love.

Recently, He told me that now is the time to battle. I don't believe this message was just for me but for every believer. Now is the time to be who He says we are, and forget who the world says we are—not out of performance, but because we have confidence in Jesus. It is time to take back what the enemy has stolen. He has been messing with our families, friends, identities, and our authority. This starts by turning to Him in prayer. I hit my knees and started to battle the enemy. My mission was to rebuke what the enemy was doing in every part of my life and to prophecy life in return. This is part of who I am now and I am getting stronger every day. His Spirit is what makes me His warrior. Now things in my life are shifting. I am contending for things in my life with the authority of Jesus, and thanks to Jesus the enemy is losing. My family has started to follow Jesus with more zeal, and my friend's lives are being radically changed. Things are starting to change all around me. I am so thankful because He so graciously showed me more of my identity. I am not living for myself but for His glory!

Chapter 2: Is Revival possible?

"With man this is impossible, but with God all things are possible" (Matthew 19:26).

We can learn so much about God's heart for revival from the story of Josiah, and many other kings in the Old Testament. But is revival possible today? We are currently seeing a Christian revival in many areas of the world. China, India, Iran, and Africa are just some of the places that are seeing large numbers of their population turn to Jesus. People in these regions are telling stories of Jesus appearing to them in dreams and visions, and even materializing before them in their homes. Some are being miraculously healed of diseases and there are even accounts of people being raised from the dead because of the faith of these converts. God is pursuing His people in great numbers, and they are responding with worship and giving Him the glory. The underground churches across many nations are growing in number, and each participant is battling fear to learn more about the Word of God, and the person of Jesus Christ.

There are few continents that are not experiencing revival, and America is one of them. Our country has for generations been blessed with prosperity and I fear it has lulled us to sleep. We worship at the altar, we verbally commit to Jesus, but where are our hearts? If you look at the Christian body, is it bringing our nation closer to our King, and representing Jesus well? There seems to be division in many churches across America, and Satan is the great divider. If he can cause us to focus on some meaningless issue, he can destroy our unity. Without unity it is hard to have power. What does Jesus want?

When Jesus came, His death fulfilled the laws and traditions of Judaism (Matthew 5:17). His goal was not to make a new system for religious people. Many of our churches here in America are described, or differentiated, by their rules or traditions. Rules and traditions can sometimes be celebrated, but often they offer false peace. A person ends up resting in the comfort in knowing they are pleasing their church rather than being spurred by a desire to please the Almighty God. The truth is, whenever we focus on rules we will struggle to live by the Spirit. Living by a list ultimately does not bring a real peace, but a poor counterfeit. Living by the Spirit always brings peace and power in abundance.

If the body of Christ is not living by the Spirit, than what is the point? I have heard many young adults ask why the church is not helping them with their identity in Christ, or addressing their deeper issues. They ask me how they could dare even start to talk about their bulimia, cutting, or sexual sins when their current church body

The body of Christ— especially young adults —deserve authentic leadership, vulnerable adults, and real conversations.

is arguing about petty things like whether someone could wear jeans to church or which type of music should be sung at the service. The body of Christ—especially young adults—deserve authentic leadership, vulnerable adults, and real conversations. Battling about some of these trivial things is bowing to the wrong God. It is time for us all to stop arguing, and start deciding to agree on the real issues. We need to seek Jesus, and let God be God. We need to dare to let the Spirit lead us, and be humble enough to listen to Him.

Many of us grew up in a religious system that focused earnestly on what a Christian should or should not do. We can have the best intentions when we do this, but it often shapes us in negative ways. Rules can be a trick by Satan to deflect our focus off of Jesus and place it on people. It can eventually breed a culture full of judgment, shame, and idolizing people. Jesus did not come to earth to patch up or fix a religious system; Jesus doesn't like religious systems. He came with His own plan. He calls us to keep our focus on Him, get to know His ways, and follow them. His gospel never changes, but He may ask us to change daily.

Do we agree that we need revival? Is there a piece of us that would like to be alive to witness great acts of God sweeping our nation? God is calling us to begin to pray for our nation, repent, and take back what Satan has stolen. He has divided our families, classrooms, courts, and even many churches. Enough already—what else are we going to hand over? It is time to fight back!

Revival of one heart is a huge deal. In recent decades there was a large move of the Spirit in Pensacola Florida that drew millions of people to a church in Brownsville. This church began to pray for revival and two years later it was estimated that 2.5 million people attended their evening services over a five year period ending in 2000.

The last time America experienced a widespread Christian revival was in the 1960's-1980's. At that point, Americans had recently had some of their most profitable decades to date. They were accustomed to a prosperous society and mostly trusted their government. But then the Vietnam War came, among other things that deflated people's impression of the America they loved. My father served in Vietnam and was one of the lucky survivors. Initially, the American populace was supportive of the war. But when their young men were coming home in body bags and the death toll continued to rise, it gave them pause.

By this time, the majority of young adults had televisions in their homes and the nightly news coverage of Vietnam and other issues sprouted distrust toward our government. Even though many of these young adults had a good childhood, they wanted something more. A prosperous lifestyle and weekly church-going were not answering their deepest questions, and they were feeling uninspired. In staggering numbers, the youth began to protest around the country and the hippie movement was born. The energy in this movement and their ability to promote change was accomplished because of their unity, passion, and focus. Unfortunately, this united group also earned a reputation for drug use, illicit sex, and rebellion.

Interestingly enough, God decided this was part of the group He wanted to use for a Christian revival. Jesus stepped into the hippie movement and started to change one soul after the next. Out of this rebellious culture Jesus changed lives and sparked a nation. The fire of the Holy Spirit spread through America and Europe, capturing person after person. I believe these young adults were chosen long before they decided to unify for certain causes. They had gifts, passions, and bravery built into their DNA for this important time. I believe the same thing about youth today.

This movement was credited for bringing new worship music to our Christian churches, and even new Christian record labels. The foundation was laid on the Word of God and its belief that a person in Christ will keep growing. Lives were challenged and changed due to the cross of Christ, and people were sold out to the cause of Jesus.

The youth of America were not the only areas experiencing revival, but were part of a movement of God that has never been seen since in our land. Americans, I am quite certain, were not deserving of this outpour. So what makes us different today?

We desire more for America. We know that we serve a great God and we long to witness His miraculous power. We each have friends and neighbors that need to be transformed by God's enduring love. Our God is never looking for the deserving, but for the wanting. The humble heart that calls out for mercy is the heart He heals. As a campus, community, or nation we can bring our requests to God for revival at this time in our history. God will hear our prayers, and mighty things will happen when we pray in unity. The fuel for revival will be first sparked in prayer. As an individual, and as a body, we need to approach the throne and pray for His mercy.

Revival is God's thing; it is not complicated, and it only requires us to be ourselves. God is not waiting for anyone specific but He will use the one who steps up. It is more about what He can do, than what we can do.

As a campus, community, or nation we can bring our requests to God for revival at this time in our history.

Let's be available to Him for a fresh revival here in America. Young adults are well able to accomplish this task. The enemy is the only thing in our way, and he can be circumvented. He is outnumbered when we unify, and nothing will be impossible for us when he is silenced. God is calling us to open our eyes to the battle around us, and fight for our nation. We only live once, let's make it count!

The Battle Plan

We all know stories of people exhibiting amazing strength. Some people are more physically strong, and we admire their athleticism at sporting events. Some others have endured terrible childhoods or actual wars, and demonstrated emotional strength that we are awed by. But the strength we need to grow in to answer God's call for revival is spiritual. When we develop spiritual strength we will cause our enemy and his army much grief. We build our spiritual muscle much like an athlete build's their physical muscles by going to the gym. Spiritual muscle is built when we focus on the spiritual realm, spend time with our King, and become empowered through the Word. We need determination, planning, and focus. In Ephesians, Paul says that we can draw encouragement on this task set before us.

> "God is strong, and he wants you strong. So take everything the Master has set out for you, well-made weapons of the best materials. And put them to use so you will be able to stand up to everything the Devil throws your way. This is no afternoon athletic contest that we'll walk away from and forget about in a couple of hours. This is for keeps, a life-or-death fight to the finish against the Devil and all his angels.

THE TIME TO TESTIFY

"Be prepared. You're up against far more than you can handle on your own. Take all the help you can get, every weapon God has issued, so that when it's all over but the shouting you'll still be on your feet. Truth, righteousness, peace, faith, and salvation are more than words. Learn how to apply them. You'll need them throughout your life. God's Word is an *indispensable* weapon. In the same way, prayer is essential in this ongoing warfare. Pray hard and long. Pray for your brothers and sisters. Keep your eyes open. Keep each other's spirits up so that no one falls behind or drops out" (Ephesians 6:10-18 MSG).

We can't start to learn about the war zone without thinking of this portion in the Bible. It is basically a call to battle. It is our orders from the General. We have all been chosen to become valiant warriors for the cause of our King. Indeed, not everyone will respond, prepare, and become a menace to Satan's evil ranks. Everything we tackle in this book, in its simplest form, is a choice. Do we want to be part of God's Special Forces here on earth, and grow spiritually strong? If we want to be stronger, we need to become more aware of the enemy and learn how to strike him where it hurts.

In this day and age Satan feels he has the edge. He has been pumping his chest and laughing with his fallen angels long enough. You can almost hear the sound of the enemy camp in almost constant celebration. Our apathetic society is clueless to the ground he is taking. How much longer are we going to rest while his demonic hoards push us around? We know Satan is sitting with a victorious grin, and raising his glass to his friends. His thirst for destruction has no end, and he is busily planning more havoc as we speak.

God is so much stronger than this menace, and He will help us bring him down. With God's mighty hand on our side the enemy will not prevail. He does not even stand a chance!

Chapter 3: Inspiration from Warriors Past

At the Colosseum's West entrance there was a gate named the Gate of Death. This is where all the dead would be carried out. Often, the families of the fighters would wait there during game days, listening to the roar of the crowd while their loved one fought. If their family member lost their battle, they could then collect the body. The dead gladiators would be stripped of his/her weapons and armor to be returned to their defeated lanista.

We can get great encouragement for battle from the warriors of the Roman Empire. Studying Rome during the time of Jesus' life on earth can give us great context for what it means to become a warrior. It is always fascinating to learn more about the culture when Jesus lived. At this time, Rome was the ruler of Judea.

Rome was very much like modern-day America. In fact, one could call them the "America" of this time period. They were rich and powerful, and were considered a threat to the known world. Their political decisions, like ours, had the potential to impact every kingdom at the time.

Rome was very much like modern-day America. In fact, one could call them the "America" of this time period.

Rome turned out inventions that helped the world prosper and were rumored to have some of the most brilliant minds among their citizens.

For example, they figured out how to have a rudimentary form of plumbing and had public baths so people did not have to bathe in the river. Wealthy Roman citizens often had their own private baths along with many ornamental fountains and gardens. Rome was one of the first civilizations to develop a type of concrete for constructing buildings and built a city that could withstand most warfare at the time. It was so strong that some of those Roman structures still stand today. They also had their own newspaper that would hang in the public forum for daily announcements.

They loved theater, fashion, and appreciated the arts. Many of the celebrities from the theater would dine with the kings and became involved in their fierce political system. The desire for power in Rome caused their five hundred senators to be full of blood-thirsty antics. Those who became part of this system found out quickly that they would need to watch their back.

Gladiators

One of the Roman citizen's favorite attractions was the deadly fights at the Colosseum. Both woman and men would fill the estimated eighty thousand seats to watch slaves fight to their last breath. They would bet money on the gladiators and would find themselves hoarse from screaming as they cheered on their favorites. One of the big imports of their day were ships full of sand to replace the sand on the Colosseum floor after a blood-washed event. Actually, the modern day word *arena* in Latin means sand.

Either the emperor or the rich would sponsor these events by paying a sum for the animals, dancers, and other entertainment to warm up the crowd. They would try to bring more creative and ferocious entertainment to avoid their own chagrin, and to appease the bloodthirsty Roman populace. Using the same aqueducts that brought water to their homes, they could even fill the arena with water to mimic a battle at sea. They were always looking for new exciting ways to watch a slave/gladiator fight to their death or be executed.

INSPIRATION FROM WARRIORS PAST

As we can surmise, this was a lucrative business. It was also a cutthroat way for a senator or citizen to move up the ladder of success, as the sponsor's favor in this affluent community was based on the crowd's excitement or boredom. If we follow the money, we can see the value in obtaining the most savage and brutal combatants from foreign crusades, whether that be animals or slaves. To find their next big star, Roman generals would often pay careful attention during the battles in foreign lands.

Of course Rome's army had some of the fiercest fighters in the world, but they were not going to subject Roman citizens to the Colosseum, unless they volunteered. So as they battled against foreign provinces, the generals of the Roman army would often search from afar to find a powerful opponent who was taking down their own soldiers. It was these amazing warriors that they would capture to take to the Colosseum as a slave to become the renowned gladiators of Rome.

Once captured, gladiators could be trained for years before fighting in their first battle. They often already had amazing skills, as did their opponents. Many of them chose to use the weapons they had trained with since youth, but some learned entirely new ones. The gladiators were often specialized at fighting other gladiators or even animals. They would be trained to use every weapon in the Roman arsenal as well as the weapons they were familiar with from their home land. Common weapons were knives, swords, harpoons, slings, and darts to name a few. Sometimes their weapon of choice could make them an authority. Surprisingly, some females trained and also battled in the ring.

Trainers would feed and train these warriors like a good horse for a race. These trainers were called lanistas. If a Gladiator had up to ten kills or more under their belt, they may become a lanista. On rare occasions, they were even freed completely and given Roman citizenship. This would usually come after they became a "star" to the citizens and were beloved. Even though these fighters were slaves, they were allowed to earn some income per fight. Apparently, they felt it motivated the warriors to have a retirement plan, so they would not use the arena as a convenient way to end their career.

Our Battle

The Bible uses fighting and warrior terminology when talking about the war that we are in against the enemy of our souls—Satan. Ephesians chapter 6 tells us to put on armor and relates each piece to a spiritual weapon that we have in our artillery. We are told that our struggle, or contest, is not against tangible opponents of flesh and blood, but against spiritual enemies. Paul tells Timothy in 2 Timothy 4:7 that he has "fought the good fight of faith," and mentions the award that he will be given, the "crown of righteousness."

If we were scheduled in the next few months to fight our enemy in the Colosseum, we would want some coaching from a lanista. We would need to memorize every tip they gave us during our training, and lean on it in battle. Since we are already waging a spiritual war, let's make truth our lanista. Satan is the father of lies, so it makes sense that truth is our greatest ammunition. Truth is the only power that can take down lies every time and set us free.

Truth is the only power that can take down lies every time and set us free.

If we were a gladiator enslaved to Rome, we would know that we have an opponent that is preparing to take us down. Today, we can be certain our adversary has been preparing for the fight against us long before our birth. We have just a short window of time to make ourselves aware of our enemy, get in the game, and defeat him. Let's get to work!

Chapter 4: A Time of Trials—Finding Healing

*"When you go to war against your enemy and see
horses and chariots and soldiers far outnumbering you,
do not recoil in fear of them; GOD, your God, who
brought you up out of Egypt is with you. When the
battle is about to begin, let the priest come forward and
speak to the troops. He'll say, "Attention, Israel,
in a few minutes you're going to do battle with your
enemies. Don't waver in resolve. Don't fear. Don't
hesitate. Don't panic. GOD, your God, is right there
with you, fighting with you against your enemies,
fighting to win" (Deuteronomy 20:1 MSG).*

One of the first things we can do to ready ourselves for battle is to give God the hurts of our past. Jesus wants us to bring them out in the light where He can bring perspective and truth that diminishes the power of hurt and brings victory to the broken places in our heart. Keeping our trials a secret only allows the enemy to make them appear bigger to us. Bringing them out into the light always brings healing. Once we give Jesus permission to take our pain, we can begin to live the full life we long for. It is hard to be in battle for others when we are not healed ourselves. Like a warrior with a wounded leg or missing limb, we find ourselves struggling. Of course, the enemy wants us to look backward at our hurts to distract and immobilize us, giving Satan's thugs more freedom to roam.

The only reason he wants us to look back is because it causes us to focus on the damage he caused in our life. He is trying to make the most of the pain he brought our way. He knows we are powerful, a warrior that can cause him much misery. Let's look up instead, and ask God for power and mercy. Even though we know God is always near, we live in a fallen world and trials are inevitable.

Job

The book of Job is the best place for us to study about how to handle brokenness. Job was a respected person in his day and age, and he had riches and blessings in abundance. The Bible tells us he owned 500 donkeys, 7,000 sheep, 3,000 camels, and 500 oxen. This was no small farm, but an absolute oasis of riches! In order to manage all that he owned, Job would have needed servants and shepherds numbering in the hundreds.

Along with riches, Job had ten children. He and his wife were blessed beyond measure. According to the book of Job, Job's children would often get together for a large feast. After these feasts Job would go out and offer burnt offerings to the Lord and beg His forgiveness, *just in case* one of his children had sinned against God in their heart. This is the kind of integrity and righteousness that Job had. We can see why he was described as blameless and upright.

One day Satan and his demons came before the Lord and asked about Job. Satan told the Lord that if Job would lose the things he loves on earth that he would surely curse God. The Lord gave Satan permission to come against Job and his family, but to not kill him. This first chapter in Job teaches us a lot about Satan. Among other things, we find that he watches believers, trying to find a way to cause us to turn our back on God. His purpose is also stated in John 10:10, saying that he comes *only* to steal, kill, and destroy.

Although Satan roams the earth and his kingdom truly can beset us, the good news is that Jesus did not just come for our salvation, but also to take back what Satan has stolen. It is stated in 1 John 3:8 that Jesus came for the purpose of destroying the works of the devil. Thankfully, Jesus has the power over death and all things evil, and that power lives in us. Yes, Satan is after us and we will be annoyed by him until he is cast into hell, but because of Jesus we are strong enough to battle this adversary. Jesus is more than a superhero, but a redeemer who desires to restore all that Satan has taken from us.

> **Jesus is more than a superhero, but a redeemer who desires to restore all that Satan has taken from us.**

As we read on in Job, we will see that in the course of just one evening, all of Job's children died while they ate together. On top of this tragic blow, in the same time period Job lost all his servants, animals, and his property was destroyed by fire. It makes me wonder if anyone in history has ever lost that much in one swoop as Job did.

When Job realized all that he had lost his response was amazing:

> "Then Job stood up and tore his robe in grief and fell down upon the ground before God. 'I came naked from my mother's womb,' he said, 'and I shall have nothing when I die. The Lord gave me everything I had, and they were his to take away. Blessed be the name of the Lord.' In all of this Job did not sin or revile God" (Job 1:20-22 TLB).

As you read the progression of Job going through this process, he tells his friends that he cursed the day of his birth, and he cursed that he was allowed to live after the day of his birth. He would rather not be born then suffer as he was. We can all feel that way when we are in trials—wondering why we were ever born into this terrible place of pain, and how we will manage to keep going. On our own, we cannot find peace and joy in our circumstances. It takes a Savior with great power to help us in our pain. Lucky for us, Jesus likes to help us out of our messes.

Naturally, Job wondered and questioned why he deserved this punishment. He knew that he was not an overt sinner and he couldn't think of anything he had done to deserve such a calamity. To make matters worse, Job got skin boils all over his body. At this point, his wife told him to "curse God and die." He responded by calling her a fool, and reminding her that we have to accept trials with the same grateful heart we accept blessings.

On our own, we cannot find peace and joy in our circumstances. It takes a Savior with great power to help us in our pain.

Trials Raise Questions

Job raises a good question. What *do* we deserve? Because we believe in a good God that loves us, does this mean we will be given everything we want? If we want to become beautiful people who are filled with compassion and love, we will not get there if we are given everything we want. So what do we deserve?

The question is not what we deserve, but what is the purpose for the trial that God is allowing in my life? Ultimately God allows things for our growth and maturity, not for our destruction. We are born with a selfish nature, which takes some true trials to get us to quit thinking about ourselves and turn towards others with love.

There are many times in the Bible that we are compared to pottery in the hands of a potter. Just like a potter can reshape a lump of clay to turn into something amazing—through a hard, twisting, and crushing process—God, the master Potter, can reshape our lives too.

> "But now, O Lord, You are our Father, we are the clay,
> and You our potter; and all of us are the work of Your
> hand" (Isaiah 64:8).

I had to go through many trials for me to see that these hard times may have actually developed something beautiful in me. Let's let the great Potter reshape us through every trial to be more like Jesus.

Another question we ask more specifically as we go through trials is, "why me?" Many times we may never get the answer to that question in our lifetime. But there are reasons for why we are facing a trial right now.

One reason for trials is simply because it is a natural consequence of being on this earth. Sin and disease have been sprinkled down the generational chain since Adam and Eve sinned in the garden. We are often the victim of someone else's sin consequence, or we may be suffering consequences from our own sin. If we know our trial is related to our own sin, the Bible tells us to humble ourselves and repent so Jesus can begin a new work in us. If we are suffering because of someone else's sin than we need to turn to God and ask for direction and comfort. It is tough when we are vicariously hurt from another person's choices. It is not always our fault that we are in pain, but it will not get better if we ignore it.

The first step for us is to work towards forgiveness. This is tough, very tough. I have prayed to have the desire to pray for someone who abused me in the past (I will share the story later in this chapter). I could not honestly say I wanted to forgive, and it made me mad that anyone would even slightly insinuate that I should. But after some contemplation and some time in God's Word, I realized that I needed to forgive. Forgiveness is not for the weak but the strong. When God helps us forgive we always realize it was for our own benefit and not our abuser's.

Forgiveness is not for the weak but the strong.

God is not asking us to stay associated with abusive people, like repeatedly approaching an electric fence and touching it. We can avoid these people. He's calling us to forgive so that we can quit carrying the hurt around. I was told long ago by a therapist that I was in a chair eating rat poison and allowing the rats to run all around me. After much time and help from God I learned that forgiveness ultimately sets us free. It allows us to get off that chair, and leave the rats behind. The *f* in forgiveness is for freedom. We can't allow our past to take down or limit our future.

THE TIME TO TESTIFY

We may never find out the real reason for our suffering. Job asks God why he is suffering, and God's answer is one of the best parts of the Bible. God does not give Job an answer, but reminds him that it is better to know God than it is to know all the answers. God simply reminds us that if we cannot understand God's great power in creation, than how do we expect to know the workings of His mind?

> "Where were you when I laid the foundations of the earth? Tell Me, if you have understanding?" (Job 38:4).

> "Have you ever in your life commanded the morning, and caused the dawn to know its place?" (Job 38:12).

> "Do you give the horse his might? Do you clothe his neck with a mane?" (Job 39:19).

> "Is it by your understanding that the hawk soars, stretching his wings toward the south?" (Job 39:26).

We will be spending eternity learning new things about God and we still will not become creators ourselves. God created and rules over everything, from microscopic things to large things that we discover only with a telescope. We can't begin to understand the working of His hands and the decisions He makes with His majesty. We need to trust that on our behalf He is in charge. As we are already saved, *we walk in eternity*. No matter what this world throws at us, we can prevail, with the help of the almighty God of this universe.

He is not a God that is absent, sleeping, or ineffective. We can call on the name of God and cry out our distress. He has the power to make the situation we are in beautiful and life-giving to ourselves and the people around us. We have no other place to turn; God alone holds the way out of trouble.

The end of Job's story is so great. Job gets all the things he lost to Satan back in abundance. The Bible says he got it all back and *doubled*!

Waiting on the Lord is not an easy place to be, but God is faithful to repay what the world has stolen from us.

If we try to imagine ourselves standing before God after our trial, what would we want it to look like? If you are like me, you would wish to handle any trial by working with God and not opposing Him, and to soar through the season with a heart of worship and gratitude for your Maker. If we could look ahead, past the current situation to the result, and see the growth that God has for us and the victory that God will deliver, we would be so much more comfortable during trials. But trials are truthfully the best place to build our trust in God. How can we tell someone else to trust Him when we can't? James says that trials should bring us joy because of the end result it produces in our lives.

> "Consider it all joy, my brethren, when you encounter various trials, knowing that the testing of your faith produces endurance. And let endurance have *its* perfect result, so that you may be perfect and complete, lacking in nothing" (James 1:2-4).

Suffering causes us to trust God for who He is, not for what He does. When we go through hardships we develop a walk with God that can't be thwarted. How else could we become a fierce soldier against Satan without prevailing in this portion of our battle? Let's allow God to heal our broken places so our relationship can build and we will not fear trials anymore. In fact, we will run to the front lines in warrior fashion and ask Him to bring it on.

When we go through hardships we develop a walk with God that can't be thwarted.

A New Perspective on Trials

When I was first awakened to the real power of God, I heard a mom saying she prays for just enough trials to keep her children close to Jesus. That blew me away. I was busy praying for constant protection around my children, and at the time I was in a place of suffering so great I felt defeated.

My enemy had me in a chokehold and probably thought He had disarmed me for life. But God gave me a victory that to this day causes my heart to sing in worship. Now I see the closeness I have gained with God because we battled together. Like warriors in battle, we build a bond with God that is unbreakable when we fight together.

I am so grateful that my Commander turned His attention to my plight during battle and caused my enemy to fall. I had been fighting him in prayer for months, and Jesus arrived just in time. There is always light in the darkness of your worst pain. When I realized that Jesus had turned the tide on my trial, I was overwhelmed and exhausted. It was time to heal my wounds. My Savior earnestly began to knit me together, and because of His love I can be a wife, mother, daughter, and friend.

I have gone through seasons where I did not have a heart of worship or gratitude. It is kind of our nature to leave Jesus out of our lives when times are good. We may still value Him, but our walk with Him becomes lackluster. God becomes like a special collector car sitting in our third stall. Something we treasure and feel is priceless, but we hardly think about it. When we go through a trial, if God were that special classic car, we do not want to leave the car for anything. We show it to everyone and go through the day gripping the wheel with all our might. If trials wake us up to our need for God and produce good fruit in abundance, then let's accept them with gladness.

> **If trials wake us up to our need for God and produce good fruit in abundance, then let's accept them with gladness.**

My Greatest Trial

My greatest trial began when I had memories resurface about being molested as a young girl by a friend of the family. Somehow I had stuck these memories in a file in my brain and they were locked up tight until about eight years ago. When these memories erupted, I thought I was going crazy. I had partly reverted back to a seven-year-old girl again. I don't know how to explain what happened to my mind, but I had crazy notions and had no idea where they were coming from.

For example, when I decided to tell my older brother Aaron about the abuse, I was afraid he would be mad at me (obviously, this is how I felt at age seven). When I went to his office to tell him, I wanted to sit on his lap. I refrained, knowing that it would be odd for a thirty-seven-year-old woman to do that, but the seven-year-old in me wanted to feel safe in my older brother's arms.

I could give you many more of these examples. I did not feel old enough to be married, or to be a mother. Part of me was operating on automatic. It took everything I had to keep it together. I'm telling you this because you need to know that circumstances can make you feel crazy and out of control. But you have a God who knows you—the deepest part of you. He promises to hold you together, and He will.

Before my flashbacks, I had quite a reputation for a few things. I was a very energetic person. I kept a very orderly home—almost perfect—and I woke up early each day to run many miles to stay in shape. People used to tease me that I did not need furniture in my home because I hardly ever sat down. These were things that I felt described me, it was who I was.

At my first therapy appointment with my husband and my mother, the therapist began to describe the traits of someone who has repressed memories like I had. Without ever knowing me, she began to describe a person who had a perfectly organized home and lots of energy all day long. She described me to a tee. Basically, all these things that I thought described me were traits from abuse. I can't explain the feeling I had when I asked her, "Who am I then?" She responded with, "We will have to wait and see." I had never felt so lost.

I felt like a beautiful vase that had fallen from a mantel and was now shattered on the floor. First of all, I felt foolish that anyone had ever thought I was "normal," and that my life up to this point had been almost completely fake. I felt like the life I built was a cover up for the real me, the hurting me that lived just underneath the surface.

Jesus showed me one piece of that shattered vase of my life at a time, and carefully glued me back together. It was a long and painful process, and I am not as beautifully put together as before, but I am stronger than ever. If it weren't for His rescue I would have ended up homeless,

I felt like a beautiful vase that had fallen from a mantel and was now shattered on the floor.

missing, or hospitalized. Now I am someone who is capable of raising my children and enjoying the blessings of being a wife, mom, mentor, and friend. When people insinuate I am a little crazy over Jesus, I have no apologies. He rescued me from a hell that I wouldn't wish on anyone. He is forever my focus and the spark of my beating heart.

I learned that in order to heal, I needed to focus on Jesus like never before. Every single time I turned backward in anger or despair, it got me nowhere. Jesus kept tenderly calling me to look at Him. It took some time for me to figure it out (and it got exhausting), but I knew that I had to count on Him to make beauty from my awful past.

Jesus used so many things to help me. His Word was water for my soul. My children were a daily reminder of why I should fight and continue to live. My husband was a rock for me, and my parents were on their knees waging a battle for me. Slowly, my despair started to lift. I remember calling my brother Dan at one point and I was crying about how much my abuser had stolen from me. He allowed me to cry it out, but then he brought a little wisdom to my pain. I remember him saying, "Satan could not touch your mercy, he could not touch your gifts." This was one of the first pieces that Jesus showed me was part of my identity—mercy. Yes, mercy! I embraced the truth of that.

At one point, God directed me to call my whole family to pray for me. He showed me that I needed help in the battle. I was too weak to carry a weapon and needed people who love me to stand between me and the enemy and wage war. I didn't realize it until this time, but I was not good at asking others for prayer. But I needed one specific miracle very badly; I needed to sleep at night. For years, I had trouble sleeping. I would often wake up screaming, believing someone was going to attack me. I would scream loud enough to scare my poor husband. It was awful because even with my eyes open I could see an attacker approaching our bed. I learned that this was a portion of my repressed memories haunting me at night. After my flashbacks, this intensified to the point that I was barely sleeping. This was when I called my whole family to pray.

Three days later, my husband ran into a woman that asked him if he knew anyone that would pray with her. It was 9:00 p.m., but my husband knew I loved to pray, so he called me and I met this lady. She immediately began to say that she didn't want to bother me so late, and I told her not to worry. I went on to say, "My husband had to wake in the middle of the night many times to pray the name of Jesus over me." When I said the name *Jesus*, a crazy thing happened. She raised her hands and went flying many feet backward off her chair like she had been punched in the stomach and said repeatedly, "Don't say that name." She began to stutter, shake, and sputter and a crazed look came over her. I knew immediately that she was filled with demons.

You would think I would be afraid, but instead I felt the power of God come over me—I swear my hair may have stood on end. I knew an angel was in the room with me, and not just any angel, a real warrior. I felt so powerful that I was afraid I could kill the woman by touching her with my pinky. It was amazing!

Our conversation went on for a while and she would sputter out Bible verses and she would cry out for healing, but at the same time she did not want her demons to leave her. After some time, I tried to walk her to her car but she did not want to be too close to me, as she could feel God's power in me. It was wild! But as I watched her drive away I realized something amazing. I knew that I was not afraid anymore.

Through this experience I am absolutely positive that we have within our reach a power greater than Satan's entire army. I cried and worshipped God that night like never before. And I am happy to report that I went home and slept like a baby.

God can use anything to bring healing to our hurt places; anything can be used for His glory. For those who may be worried about this poor woman, I know she has visited a pastor a few times and I believe that when she is willing to let go of the demons, they will be cast out. I have faith that she will be healed someday.

My final thought about trials is this: With God's help, eventually you quit asking why they happen to you. You forgive your abusers, realizing that Satan is the real problem. You count it a blessing that God can take something so painful and allow you to use it to encourage others.

I am a living example of an unworthy person who has been rebuilt by God's good hands. I am not a picture of what a human can do, but of what God can do. By His power I wake each day with a sound mind and a heart of worship. He wants to do this for all of us.

Do you think Job realized that his story would encourage masses of people thousands of years later? How many lives were held together because of his story? When Job finally stood before God I bet he was surprised to have pictured us reading about him. I have the feeling that Job would not change his earthly life now, not for anything.

Meet Allison Jahn
Aspiring Worship Leader/Song Writer
Recent Graduate of the University of Nebraska

I have walked through so many seasons of life where it feels like everything is going up in flames. The most important lesson I have learned during these times is that those seasons are gifts from God. In order to see them as gifts it is crucial to be grounded in truth; to *know His character*, and to trust His heart. In Matthew 6:26, Jesus reminds us that the Father provides for the birds of the air, and if we are of more value than them, how could He not provide for our needs as well? He is a Father that gives *good* gifts to His children, and this truth allows me to believe He is always working for my good. I began to see how every trial is for my good and can make my faith stronger. Trials can be used to purify my heart for Him, and to teach me to run after Him all the more. Trials reveal my weaknesses and need for His Spirit. If we trust His heart, know His love, and seek Him above all, we will be assured that He is for us no matter what comes our way. It will be worth it!

Meet Cash Rodamaker
Junior at Bethel University
St. Paul, Minnesota

I grew up with my mom and sister in the Minneapolis area. My parents got divorced when I was four and I would visit my dad every other weekend as a child. I was broken as I grew up, missing identity and security. In spite of this, I began to excel in sports, and this led to popularity in school and my identity was formed from this. I was selfish, verbally abusive, and lost. When we moved to the suburbs I was introduced to a youth group. Church hadn't been my thing up to this point, but I decided to try it out anyway.

In 8th grade I went to a church retreat, and after listening to a message about making God the center of your life, I stood up to leave. Suddenly I felt this overwhelming urge to sit down and pray. This was new to me. As I sat there, I asked God, "Who are you? Is any of this even real?" At that moment, I was overtaken by the Holy Spirit. I began to weep and tremble. It felt like a wave of pure joy, love, peace, and emotion crashed over my heart. I had never felt anything like it in my life. From there, everything took a 180 degree turn. Life was no longer about me and my accomplishments, but about living to glorify a good God.

God began to teach me who He was and what living for Him looked like. I would ask God questions and then flip to a random page in the Bible and miraculously the answer would be on that very page. One time God told me to go up to someone and tell her that she was amazing.

THE TIME TO TESTIFY

I did what God told me to do and as I began to speak, the Holy Spirit took me over and spoke directly to her heart. It was life changing for her, and super cool to witness. God showed me His power to perform miraculous healings when I saw someone who tore his ACL just days prior to receiving prayer, throw his crutches into the air and run around the sanctuary with a smile. I will never forget that. By God's grace, I began to see the Holy Spirit dramatically change people's lives. I grew in boldness, passion, love, and wisdom. By the time I was a junior in high school I started to mentor people and I was known as someone to come to if you needed help. This was an amazing time in my life and such a testament to God's grace, but there is another side to the story.

In John 10:10 it says, "The thief comes only to steal and kill and destroy." And that's what he did. When I was in 7th grade, I was first exposed to pornography. It felt wrong, but right at the same time. By the time I became a Christian, it was already a regular part of my life. Every chain in my life fell off after I gave my life to Christ. Or so I thought. Pornography didn't leave. The more I grew in my faith the bigger a burden this became. I would ask God, "Why don't you take this away? It's killing me!" The more I grew to love God, the more shame I felt for this continuous sin. I loved God and wanted to do what was right, but there was this serious pull towards death. Why?

As the months, then years, of this addiction continued, I started to feel numb. At night it would be the only subject God and I talked about. No matter what happened that day, my "faith" became based upon the occurrence of one sin. I believed in a God who loved me unconditionally, but also believed that I only deserved His love when I didn't sin. I would read Romans 7 when Paul says, "For the good that I want, I do not do, but I practice the very evil that I do not want." But then he continues to write about where his deliverance comes from, "Thanks be to God through Jesus Christ our Lord!" At this I would feel sick to my stomach and say, "God, I don't feel 'delivered.' Where did I go wrong?" On the outside, everything looked like I was on track to become a youth pastor (if that was

God's plan). But the truth was that every compliment I received for my "amazing faith in God" was like a knife gently forced into my side. If only they knew what I actually did—who I actually was. I would think, *God where are you in this?*

Finally, after seven years God spoke to me in a whisper, "Cash, you're asking Me to do something that was already accomplished two thousand years ago on a cross." So by God's grace the thing that finally set me free from my addiction was the most fundamental facet of Christianity—the gospel. When Jesus died for my sin, God knew the full weight of what that meant. He bore the entirety of my sin. Everything I have ever done and will ever do. Because of Jesus, God says I am righteous, flawless, sinless, and holy. Faith in Christ doesn't just mean believing in what He did, but believing who I am in light of what He did. No matter what "sin" I fall to, nothing about who I am changes. When sin doesn't change your identity, it loses its power over your life. This was the truth I needed so that pornography would finally lose its power over my life. Because of God's grace, I was finally *free*!

Now, this grace isn't a "get-out-of-jail-free" card. Jesus didn't bear the weight of our sin just to convince us to love God. He bore our sin because a sinful humanity cannot be reconciled to relationship with a Holy God. He bore our sin to enable us to participate in a loving relationship with our Father. I am invited into a life of living out this truth. My flesh and soul, though united, are at absolute odds. Satan is working against me daily, but I am not my flesh, and I am not a slave to evil. There is no condemnation for those who are in Christ Jesus. I am a son of God made eternally righteous. I now get to live my life pressing into this truth which will eventually be made complete when Christ Jesus returns.

> "I have come that they may have life, and have it to the full" (John 10:10b NIV).

THE TIME TO TESTIFY

Meet Jenna Meyers
Freshman at University of Minnesota
Minnesota Gopher Dance Team Member
Minneapolis, MN

When people think of joy, they often think of someone with a smile on their face or someone beaming with content, but it is so much more than that. There is such a difference between being happy and the overwhelming excitement of joy. *Joy* can be a state of being. Happiness is so temporary and fleeting. Joy is caused by something so much greater than winning a gold medal or celebrating your birthday; it is caused and given freely by our heavenly Father above. He is exceptionally good and completely satisfying. When we feel empty and ask Him to fill us up, He will not only fill us but give everything we need in abundance. He will fill our cup so full it is bound to splash on others. We can never run dry because our Father is eternal and will continue to always fill our lives and hearts with elation. I am not saying that you won't ever be sad, mad, upset, or cry. But it is possible to find joy, even in the tears, because our God Almighty makes the impossible possible! He wants us to find joy in the dark times, and in the times of surrender. He wants us to find joy in the frustrating times, and in the times of a trial set before us. He especially wants us to find joy in the times of celebration, rejoicing, and love! So do not lean on this world to find yourself at that temporary state of being "happy," but seek for something far greater, because Jesus wants to give it to us. His heart is filled with joy when our hearts are filled with joy as well.

> "Rejoice in the Lord always; again I will say, rejoice" (Philippians 4:4).

Chapter 5: No Time for Shame—Embracing Grace

If a gladiator gained the sympathy of Rome's fans by winning many battles, they were eventually offered a Rudis by the Emperor. This Rudis allowed them to walk through the East gate called the Gate of Life and be a free Roman citizen. It is believed they were offered the small wooden sword so they wouldn't immediately take their long-boiling frustration out on a group of unarmed Roman citizens.

A nother way that we suffer in battle is when we are looking at our past in shame. Shame disarms us and makes us believe that we are not worthy for battle. We start labeling ourselves by our mistakes and not by our true identity, and we walk in the wrong armor. Instead of the armor of truth and righteousness we dress in thin rags. How the enemy loves to show us a mirror and trick us to search our past for our identity. He has to be silenced. The battleground is in our minds, so let's start fighting back and focus our minds on the truth. Wrong beliefs about our own worth can feel impossible to unwind but it can be done. Lies are like spider webs in our mind; when we throw a few pebbles at it, they fall apart. Truth is a wall of marble. Once firmly set into place it is hard to move. We need to see our past through the lens of grace. God's grace reclaims our past and challenges us to love ourselves as He loves us. Embracing His definition of ourselves gives us

THE TIME TO TESTIFY

a new foundation to stand on and it supplies us with ammunition for the enemy's next attack. Let's rework our identities together.

The Power of Words

An amazing thing happened in 1980. I was eleven years old when twenty American college-age kids took to the ice and defeated the Soviets in the semi-final ice hockey game in the Olympics. You may have heard of this notable win, but in context of our history it was much more than a hockey game.

At the time of this Olympics, our country was just starting to struggle with the belief that the American way was working. We were in a gas crisis that left long lines at the pump each day. We feared nuclear attack, and after suffering through so many years of the Cold War we were feeling defeated. Our outlook was dimming, and we were becoming fearful for the future of our great nation.

We were somewhat afraid of the Soviets at the time. The media portrayed them not as natural humans, but machines. I remember practicing curling under my desk at school in case of a bomb attack, and it made my heart race every time. Times were different then. The only images we had of the Soviets were the scraps we got on the nightly news. We did not have the internet, thus we were limited for information to put things in perspective.

What these twenty kids accomplished was truly unbelievable. Our NHL All-Star team had played the Soviets only a few months prior to the Olympics and lost to them 6-1. This Soviet team had won the gold medal the last four Olympics, and looked like they may become international superstars again. There was only one man that thought the Soviets were beatable, and that was Herb Brooks. He is a legend here in Minnesota. Herb believed that we could win if he combined the right team. As their coach, he was not looking for great hockey players, but players with certain gifts. This reminds me of how God sees us. When He chooses a good team He combines many gifts together for the best team possible.

NO TIME FOR SHAME—EMBRACING GRACE

No matter how trivial we feel, there is a ministry or team out there that needs us to show up and use our gifts.

On the night of the Olympic game against the Soviets, the pre-game locker room was pretty quiet. I can only imagine how nervous they were. These boys had gotten a chance to play the Soviets just before the Olympics and lost 10-3. This is when Herb gave an incredible speech,

No matter how trivial we feel, there is a ministry or team out there that needs us to show up and use our gifts.

that gives me chills every time I hear it, and is a reminder to me of the power of words in our lives. This is especially true about the power of words spoken over us by someone we look up to and trust.

Here is what Herb said, "Great moments are born from great opportunity, and that's what you have here tonight, boys. That's what you've earned here tonight. One game; if we played them ten times, they might win nine. But not this game, not tonight. Tonight, we skate with them. Tonight we stay with them, and we shut them down because we can. Tonight, we are the greatest hockey team in the world. You were born to be hockey players—every one of you, and you were meant to be here tonight. This is your time. Their time is done. It's over. I'm sick and tired of hearing about what a great hockey team the Soviets have. Screw 'em. This is your time. Now go out there and take it!"[1]

This team went out and beat the Soviet's 4-3. Some call it the biggest upset in sports history. I remember my dad and a couple friends watching the game. I can still picture them off their chairs yelling at the TV as if the game was costing them their very lives. When we won, the release of excitement in the room was tangible. Herb ignited an unstoppable fire, and its effect turned fear into faith across our nation. This is an example of just one person's faith-filled words, spoken in a secular setting. How much more could God use us all if we could commit to do His will together?

---

1. Herb Brooks, 1980.

THE TIME TO TESTIFY

Whether we are friends, roommates, neighbors, or relatives we have used words either to encourage or discourage people. We have all heard a mix of these through the years, and these words weave our self-perception for the good or the bad. When we were infants we were innately certain that we have value. As toddlers, our favorite word was *mine*, and the early years of elementary school are partly spent teaching us to take turns and share.

When my son Bradley was six years old he prayed God would send him a neighbor friend. I was praying alongside of him, and afterwards he looked at me and asked if the new friend would come over today. I explained in all my "wisdom" that we often have to wait on God. Well, two hours later a mom stopped by with her son Travis, who was Bradley's age. Travis was even holding a bag of candy to share with Bradley. I could not believe my eyes. I was so grateful to God for showing Bradley how much He cares for him. But I guess I needed that lesson more than Bradley did. It was the best humbling moment ever.

So how do we go from thinking we are special to God to wondering if we have value at all? How do we get to the point where we feel like garbage, and even consider suicide? We need to realize that every message we receive about ourselves that is contrary to God's truth is damaging. These words should never be taken lightly—they become shackles on our ankles, and they eventually are a stronghold on our minds. We need to remember that Satan came *only* to kill, steal, and destroy. Words are one of his weapons, and he is a master at lying. He never tells the truth! Let's devise a defensive plan against this game of his. We are already in a battle here on earth. One of his greatest tactics against us is rooted in the lie of shame.

The fact about shame is that when we are overcome by it, we become immobile in our crusade. When we make a poor decision we might feel guilty, but that is not the same as shame. Guilt says that we *made* a mistake. Shame says that we *are* the mistake.

When someone sins, it should not reflect on that person as a whole. We can look back at choices we made and feel somewhat guilty, but shame leads us to feel broken, or unfixable, and leads us to a place of hopelessness. Any message that we are not good enough, pretty enough, smart enough, or strong-willed enough to make it in this world can turn into these scandalous feelings. These damaging words will often become repeating messages that alter our true identity as God's own children.

Some people can feel chagrined because of their past mistakes. Interestingly, our Father doesn't even remember our sin, but we can't seem to erase it from our minds. The Liar wants us to think that God loves us less when we sin, and more when we walk in truth. The fact is that He loves us the same. He does not love the saint more than the murderer. God does not love us because of who we are, but because of who He is. God is love.

The more we reflect on our past wrongdoings, the more we miss out on the joy set before us. If we have shame knit into our identity we can make choices from these lies at times. We can get caught up in sin because we don't feel we are worth the effort of good choices. Deep down these feelings are rooted in lies. So let's get to the truth of the matter and start kicking shame to the curb. To do this we need to start from the beginning. First let's talk about who we truly are.

> "God spoke: 'Let us make human beings in our image, make them reflecting our nature'" (Genesis 1:26 MSG).

> "[God] shows no partiality to princes nor regards the rich above the poor, for they all are the work of His hands" (Job 34:19).

God made the entire universe and the many billions of creations that fill it. All the earth was made to sustain life and give us resources in abundance. His creations were made to bring Him

We are not a random creation; but a chosen, detailed, and intentional creation.

glory and bless us. The cool part about it all is that God saved us as His greatest creation. We were made in His image, and are each His glorious masterpiece. We were specifically chosen to be human; not an angel, and not an animal. We are human beings. We are not a random creation; but a chosen, detailed, and intentional creation.

What would it be like to live every day knowing that the Creator of humanity calls us "very good"? It would transform the way we think and live, especially the view we have of ourselves. He has literally knit us with the very best intentions to reflect His image and His glory. When we embrace this reality, we can see that saying anyone's image, including our own, is "less than good" really brings hurt to the Creator because we are critiquing His perfect work. It would be beneficial to stop the gerbil wheel in our minds and refuse to think poorly of ourselves.

Did you know that thoughts can be rewired? Scientifically, our brain has neurons that react to stimuli in our mind. These neurons pick up our habits and make pathways in our brain to make the processing even faster. Pathways are a great gift when they help us do two things at once. But when they go awry it can be hard to untangle. Rerouting these messages can give us freedom like never before.

We need to fight with all our might not to criticize ourselves.

Clearing these back alleys in our mind takes work, but is worth the effort. We need to listen to the words that come out of our lips or zing through our brain and stop them. Some of us may have to go on a fast from even speaking out loud. Not as a punishment, but as an action that will create a better habit. We need to fight with all our might not to criticize ourselves. Renewing our mind and making new pathways is tough, but it is so important to give it our all.

> "The words of a wise person are gracious. The talk of a fool
> self-destructs—he starts out talking nonsense and ends up
> spouting insanity and evil" (Ecclesiastics 10:12 MSG).

No Time for Shame—Embracing Grace

If we spend time savoring a fool's words about us, it can honestly drive us mad. Who cares what some bad person says about us when we know that God adores our every part? There comes a point when we have to realize that we will never be good enough for certain people. But is that our problem or theirs?

Everyone has strengths and weaknesses. Interestingly, our limitations are not a mishap. God has chosen our gifts and our weaknesses with equal precision and both are areas of our lives in which we can choose to dedicate to Him.

However, our limitations can be a breeding ground for shame, so we have to be careful not to allow this to happen. Where we see limitations, God sees a place for us to lean on Him. We should not be hard on ourselves because we were not created perfect. Our Creator chose to make us just as we are. God did not give us shortcomings so we could shame ourselves. What if we decided to praise God for these areas that force us to rely on His strength and further our intimacy with Him?

When we sin, we need to ask God for forgiveness and receive His grace. His grace abounds for hearts that repent. A heart of repentance is one of the most beautiful things we can bring Him. He always has mercy to grant us and longs to help us overpower our temptations. He promises to help make our paths straight and give us grace for every mile and minute along the way. God's grace is the greatest undeserved gift we will receive on earth. He longs to pour it out and repair our broken places.

> **God's grace is the greatest undeserved gift we will receive on earth.**

Once we are washed in the blood of Christ and forgiven of our sins, God no longer sees them anymore. He sees us as blameless, and righteous—not because of what we have done, but because Jesus stands as our great Defender. At this point we cannot listen to the enemy who wants us to look back at what we have done, but receive the grace granted to us. Only then can we approach our next moments as victors.

We need to picture the Colosseum after we are victorious. We would receive the wreath of a champion, bow before our King, and press on with power and might. Once we have beat our adversary at this part of his game, we won't fall for it so easily again. We may need to distance ourselves from the people that cause us to feel that way until God replaces the shame with our true identity.

Luckily Truth, or Jesus, is our lanista. He is the great Healer who grants life. He has already defeated the enemy and we are risen above Satan because of Him. He has the power that created the universe at His disposal, and is ready to unleash it when we ask. He may decide to take the lies from us and make us new in an instant. Sometimes He works that way. But most things in our life need to be removed slowly.

There are three key weapons that we need to understand and be trained to use as we stand in the dirt of the Colosseum. They are the weapons we need to use against our enemy.

Jesus' Name

We never want to go into any crusade without the name of Jesus. The Bible tells us that there is power in the name of Jesus. We can use this capability as His son or daughter and begin to reclaim our thoughts. In the Word it says that God gave Jesus the name above all names. This must mean that any other name falls below Jesus and *must* yield to Him. So Jesus' name is above any human name. It is greater than the name Daisy, Conrad, Viktor, or Angie. It is also greater than the name Hitler or Osama. There is no name on earth that can harm your eternal being. Jesus' name has power over all human names.

Jesus' name has power over names we have called ourselves, or have been called. Names like idiot, stupid, freak, misfit, clown, ugly, dweeb, addict, garbage, weirdo, druggie, stoner, hooker, slut, whore, player, nerd, and loner need to flee in Jesus' name.

The name of Jesus is above the name of Jesus, bulimia, depression, epilepsy, diabetes, and every other disease. There is no prayer on earth that does not need the power of Jesus'

There is nothing that can come against us that Jesus' name can't handle.

name prayed through it. There is nothing that can come against us that Jesus' name can't handle. Even the demons tremble at His name. We need to use it. We don't use guns and bullets to fight the enemy. We use this name: *Jesus*, a powerful word. It is the nuclear bomb of the spiritual world!

> "The name of the Lord is a strong tower; the righteous run into it and it is safe" (Proverbs 18:10).

> "For this reason also, God highly exalted Him, and bestowed on Him the name which is above every name, so that at the name of Jesus every knee will bow, of those who are in heaven and on earth and under the earth" (PHILIPPIANS 2:9-10).

Jesus' Blood

Because of the blood of Jesus and its power over redemption, we already reside in eternity. Satan is beneath our feet, and we are spiritually with Jesus. When our spirit is reborn into God's kingdom, we are now citizens of heaven even though we still live physically on earth. If you have ever spent an intimate time with Jesus, you know that it can be hard to come back and engage here on earth. It is like you get caught up in the heavenly realm and are almost fully there, but physically here. We can't grasp it, and we don't totally understand it, but we are already seated far above our adversary.

It is also because of the blood of Jesus that we are forgiven. It was the sacrifice that redeemed all of mankind. Once our sins have been washed with the blood of Christ they can no longer demand our attention. Our mistakes do not define us, our Father does. We are precious and loved because He loves us.

Our mistakes do not define us, our Father does. We are precious and loved because He loves us.

The Word

Along with the name of Jesus and His blood, we can use Scripture to rewire our brains. We may not know all the addresses of the verses, but we need to memorize the Word.

> "God means what he says. What he says goes. His powerful Word is sharp as a surgeon's scalpel, cutting through everything, whether doubt or defense, laying us open to listen and obey. Nothing and no one is impervious to God's Word. We can't get away from it—no matter what" (Hebrews 4:12-13 MSG).

Memorizing Scripture will help us distinguish when we are being lied to by Satan, people, or even our self. We will gain discernment that will help us moment by moment. But, mostly we will combat the deceptions in our spirit one by one. Satan may not leave us alone completely until Jesus returns, but metaphorically we can have him pinned to the ground.

> "I have hidden your word in my heart, that I might not sin against you" (Psalm 119:11 NLT).

A Letter from God

Effectively rewiring our brain will be easier by using these three things that Jesus provides. Because we have the Holy Spirit living in us, we have constant access to Jesus. Let's not walk into the ring without the only weapons that can give us the advantage.

I want to share a letter that I felt God gave to me. I have read this so many times that I have it memorized. It has helped set me free from shame and enabled me to embrace the grace of my Father.

NO TIME FOR SHAME—EMBRACING GRACE

Dear Child,

Do not measure yourself by the measure of the carnal minded, but begin to measure yourself by My measure. I created you and I call you by name. It is by my perfect design that you hold certain noticeable gifts.

Do not judge yourself by your limitations. Your limitations are also chosen by Me as an opportunity for us to do things together. See your limitations as opportunities to lean on Me, so when you stand before me we will already be friends.

Of all creation, from the ants in the fields to the elephants of Africa, and from the coral reefs of Australia to the distant star in the sky—you are the only creation I desire to commune with every day.

The detail in your eyes show more workmanship than the planets that surround earth, and give you distinction for all eternity. No other human created has your eyes!

You should not look in the mirror to always find something to change, but also to behold one of My greatest creations!

Do not allow the shame of your past to wash over you at every turn. Counter it with truth and walk in My grace.

For I have already told you what is best—to love mercy, use good judgement, and walk closely with Me.

I focus on the desire of your heart and not your actions. I continue to delight in you, even when you make a mistake.

I see progress when you often see failure.

I see true work ethic and determination where you continue to see barriers.

I see your weakest point as a place to join you, and you see that as a place that defines you.

Begin to see yourself as I see you today, and give Me the authority I deserve. I have called you good, perfect, holy, redeemed, beloved, and most of all, *Mine*.

Love, Jesus

Herb Brooks' speech deserves a rewrite for our battle:

Transformation can happen every day, and that's what we have here by God's grace, guys! That's what God offers you each and every night! But tonight; I am begging you to let God take your mind tonight. If you still desire, you can go back to your old ways tomorrow. But not right now, not tonight. Tonight we are going to accept the truth. Tonight we are going to fight for truth. And we are going to shut Satan down, because we can. Tonight you are the valuable child of the Most High God. You were born to be His Child—every one of you, and you were meant to be here tonight. This is your time! Your enemy's time is done. It's over. I am sick and tired of hearing you return to your old lies about yourself. Screw 'em. This is your time. Now go out there and claim it!

A few verses to put to memory:

"Just as He chose us in Him before the foundation of the world, that we would be holy and blameless before Him. In love, He predestined us to adoption as sons through Jesus Christ to Himself, according to the kind attention of His will" (Ephesians 1:4).

"Therefore, confess your sins to one another, and pray for one another so that you may be healed. The effective prayer of a righteous man can accomplish much" (James 5:16).

"Do not fear, for I have redeemed you; I have called you by name; you are Mine!" (Isaiah 43:1b).

No Time for Shame—Embracing Grace

"Therefore you are no longer a slave, but a son; and if a son, then an heir through God" (Galatians 4:7).

Meet Olivia Emer
Sophomore at Bethel University
St. Paul Minnesota

For many years I struggled with lust. This sin started hurting my true identity because I let shame overwhelm me. Living in shame trapped me from continuing my journey with The Lord. It chained me to my sin and told me, "This is what you've done and this is who you are." But the grace that God so graciously gave me shattered those words and broke my chains. The Lord continues to remind me that He sees me through the eyes of grace. I have learned that I need to look at myself the way my Father looks at me, then I feel new. And that feeling of newness makes me want to live out my true identity, free from lust. Walking in His grace brings me freedom, and there is no room for shame anymore.

> "Therefore, there is now no condemnation for those who are in Christ Jesus, because through Christ Jesus the law of the Spirit who gives life has set you free from sin and death" (Romans 8:1-2 NIV).

Meet Ryan Ylitalo
Freshman at The University of Minnesota
Minneapolis, Minnesota

Shame and guilt have no association so don't be confused about this. Guilt is something we naturally feel when we do something wrong. This is a bad feeling, but quite normal. Guilt should lead us to turn to God for forgiveness. But whatever the sin may be, you should never feel shameful about yourself, who you are, or about your relationship with God. Shame never comes from God. Rejoice in peace and grace, and do not let Satan's ploy of shame hold you back. The penalty has been paid and the battle has already been won. God's grace is infinite, and your

67

relationship is not damaged by the sins you commit, because His love for you does not waver based on your actions. His love is everlasting while this life is temporary. So when you feel guilt, accept that you are forgiven, put your chin up, and move on. Shame is the last thing anyone needs. You are loved, cared for, forgiven, and perfect in His eyes.

Chapter 6: The Moment of Temptation— Avoiding the Trap

One famous gladiator named Flamma was offered the Rudis four times, but continued to be a gladiator. It is believed that he was originally captured in Syria. He was literally an idol in the city of Rome. He eventually fell in his thirty-fourth battle at the age of thirty. It is recorded that he won twenty-one battles, had nine end in a draw, and was beaten four times. Apparently, he was spared three of those times because the public could not bear to grieve his loss.

We don't have to think too hard to name a movie that plays off of the role between darkness and light. We could list countless stories that illustrate a battle between evil and good. At our very core we can relate to this battle because we walk in it every day. We all face temptations in different areas and it is tough to fight them. We can harbor hatred for people and wish revenge on our enemies. We gossip, lie, walk in pride, and choose sin over good time and time again. Each of us has a story that could be knit into the silver screens of today's theaters.

It is interesting how we all know that it will not end well for a character in a movie who claims to be God or asks people to bow to them. Pride is one of God's most hated sins, and it is the typical enticement of Satan. When he tempted Eve in the garden of Eden, she was not that enticed

69

about eating some fruit. She could have all the fruit she wanted! The real draw was knowledge that she did not yet possess. Satan knew Eve's weakness and convinced her that if she ate of the tree of life she would be like God and have full knowledge of good and evil.

He is a crafty tempter, a total pest. I can't remember a day where I was not excited about fighting Satan. At about the age of five I used to love to picture his face on the floor and jump on it. Somehow, I innately knew that he was my adversary. I often pray that when Satan is cast into hell, that God would let me give him a swift kick in the butt! This desire is probably because of my abuse as a child. I have seen what Satan can do to people and the destruction that he craves to create in our lives. He is the great divider, always looking to bring division to marriages, families, friendships, and especially in the body of Christ.

I have noticed that people avoid talking about the dark world and often act as though it doesn't exist. This is Satan's greatest trick. If he can convince you that he does not exist, then he can catch you off guard. I promise he is active on this earth. The story of Satan starts in Genesis and goes through Revelations. He is mentioned directly over a hundred times in the Bible, and countless times indirectly. Some people wrongly believe that Satan is an equal to God, but they do not realize that Satan was actually created by God. The Devil hasn't ever created anything, he is not omniscient and can't discern our thoughts. Even though he is the biggest liar of all time, we don't need to bow to his ways.

We can stand with the armor of God, and prevail against him with God's power. We have no reason to fear. We just need to get real about the battle were in so we don't walk in defeat through life. There is no time for apathy or sleepwalking anymore—our nation **When we recognize his influence in our own life, we will recognize it in our nation.** has done that long enough. The time has come for us to recognize the battle zone around us and fight. Together we can push back the enemy. When we recognize his influence in our own life, we will recognize it in our nation. We will not regret girding up for war, it will bring us the fearless faith of giants, and bring blessings for ourselves and the next generation.

> "Put on all of God's armor so that you will be able to stand firm against all strategies of the devil. For we are not fighting against flesh-and-blood enemies, but against evil rulers and authorities of the unseen world, against mighty powers in this dark world, and against evil spirits in the heavenly places" (Ephesians 6:11-12 NLT).

Living in the War Zone

The truth is that we were conceived and born into a war zone. This is not a war we can avoid, or decide to abandon. It is around us whether we choose to look for it or not. Satan is our adversary, but is ultimately not after us, he is after God. God is on our side, and His power can be used to circumvent the enemy and give us peace in abundance. But let's learn to avoid Satan's schemes.

In the Roman Colosseum, there were sixteen inches of fresh sand on top of a wood base. The wood base contained trap doors that would allow the sponsor to introduce surprises during a fight. The goal was to provide a show with creative twists and keep the crowd on the edge of their seats. The trap doors were one of the audience's favorite parts, as they could be used to escalate up the action when a fight got boring. The criminals and slaves that were sentenced to death needed to beware, because they were often the ones who were surprised by the trapdoors. For example, during the battle a slave could be enticed to fight a small animal, only to find out that a hungry lion or pack of dogs had been released from the floor behind him.

This metaphorically reminds me of the traps our minds engage in when we step into trouble. A simple decision to lie, gossip, or steal can quickly turn into a much bigger problem. The small enticements of our flesh are not something to minimize. How do we get our head in the game and avoid the trapdoors?

The first step in avoiding trouble is to recognize that we are born with an appetite for sin. We need to remember that we can be deceived and admit we need protection, truth, and direction.

In 1 John 1:10 it says that, "If we say that we have not sinned, we make Him a liar and His word is not in us." We all make mistakes and bring hurt to people around us with great consequences. It is our natural bend.

But we don't usually sin out of nowhere. It starts with a temptation or thought that entices us, drawing our attention.

It would be so amazing if we could analyze our thoughts and cast out our temptations instantly. The Bible says to take our thoughts captive and really think about what we are tempted to do (2 Corinthians 10:5). This means to ask ourselves what could be a possible consequence to this choice? Is it legal? Is it against God's law? Could it ruin our reputation? God adores us, but He does allow consequences to come our way when we sin.

My father was an alcoholic. He started drinking after Vietnam and was instantly overboard. He spent a few years under the influence before seeking treatment. However, the consequences of his addiction did not stop with him, it affected all of the family. I believe my dad would not have taken a drink if he could have seen the havoc it would cause our family. But when we are tempted our thinking becomes cloudy. My father saw a trapdoor with a drink that he felt would make him happy, but he never saw the monster of addiction closing in on him from behind.

We need to bring our thoughts to Jesus. God has promised that He always allows a way out from sin, that He will not tempt us, and does not throw trouble in our path as some sort of game or test. This is not the God we serve.

> "No test or temptation that comes your way is beyond the
> course of what others have had to face. All you need to

remember is that God will never let you down; he'll never let you be pushed past your limit; he'll always be there to help you come through it" (1 Corinthians 10:13 MSG).

I have talked to many people who feel they need to repent of the trouble they have been in. Feeling the need to repent can be a very vulnerable place. When people come to me to talk about their issues, I consider it a privilege to be someone they feel safe to "dump" on. I will often ask them if they can think of a "way out" that God gave them that they refused. Every single time, they have answered yes. I know from experience that "gut feeling" that there is something I have ignored when I have decided to sin. Why do we deny it?

Popularity and acceptance can drive a lot of our actions. Peer pressure can spur our thinking and literally trap us. Before long, we feel that we have to participate in something we never thought we would do. How do we battle these things?

> **Popularity and acceptance can drive a lot of our actions. Peer pressure can spur our thinking and literally trap us.**

We need to seek God's ways above everything else. When God is not at the center of our life, our thinking becomes foolish. We begin to look for acceptance and importance in others. Sin is a slow change as it roots into our hearts, eventually turning our attention from our King to something else. Somehow we go from God-focused to self-focused.

> "God cannot give us happiness and peace apart from Himself because it is not there. There is no such thing."
> – C.S. Lewis

Let's always remember to place Jesus on the throne of our life. He is not trying to boss us around, He is trying to help us have a blessed life. Let's get our eyes fixed on Him and follow Him with persistence. He is the best friend we could ever find! Learning to listen to His voice instead of our flesh will give us an advantage over sin.

Busted

I want to talk about a big bust that is in the Bible. For those of you who may not be as familiar with the life of King David, I will give you a little background. King David was the son of Jesse and was raised with seven older brothers. We can find his complete story from 1 Samuel through 2 Kings.

When David was just a young teenager he was chosen over his older and mightier brothers to be the next king of Israel. In spite of being smaller and slighter than them, God wanted David to be the next king. When the prophet Samuel came to the home of Jesse to anoint the next king as requested by God, even he was stunned to see who God had chosen. God told Samuel not to look at the stature of the other brothers because He had rejected them, and that He was not looking at David's physical appearance, but his heart. Our Father gives such a sweet picture of the type of person He wants to raise up; someone who enjoys worshipping Jesus and whose heart delights in doing good. This was David as a boy. This is the same David that defeated Goliath.

David eventually became king over Israel and grew to be a great ruler. But like us, he had weaknesses that could bring him down. One of David's weaknesses was lust; especially for one woman who totally clouded his thinking. You would think this was a storyline from a modern-day movie!

One day as David's army was out fighting a war, he was walking along the roof of his home. He saw a woman bathing and thought she was gorgeous. He sent a servant to figure out who she was, and found out that her name was Bathsheba, the wife of Uriah the Hittite, who happened to be fighting a battle in David's army.

Uriah was one of David's most loyal warriors. I think God allowed this information as a way out, a moment for David to think about returning Uriah's loyalty would have been very wise right now. But David called for her anyway and had sex with her. Some theologians complain about Bathsheba, saying she probably seduced David, but I believe she was probably obeying her earthly king. To refuse a king in those days was to risk your life. To David's surprise, weeks later Bathsheba sends him a little message; three little words that sent his life off course, "I am pregnant."

David could have owned up to everything at this point. But admitting to adultery would have given him the death penalty. So what does David do? Instead of coming clean, David has Uriah brought back from fighting and invites him over for dinner. His plan was to get him drunk and have him go lay with Bathsheba, thus making it look like the baby was Uriah's. But Uriah does not want to be intimate with his wife when his men are out risking their lives at war, so he refuses. This again displays Uriah's great character.

Now David's plan gets a little stickier. What are his choices now? He could be truthful and die, or he could deny having sex with Bathsheba. But that could cost Bathsheba her life because Uriah would know that she had been unfaithful. David doesn't do either of these things, but much worse, he sends Uriah back to the war zone and asks him to carry a message to Joab who was the commander at the time. The letter Uriah carried to Joab was actually Uriah's own death sentence.

> "Put Uriah in the front lines where the fighting is the fiercest. Then pull back and leave him exposed so that he's sure to be killed" (2 Samuel 11:15b MSG).

David probably figured, "If I get rid of Uriah we can just claim the baby is Uriah's and pretend he had sex with her the evening I had him come home from battle." After Uriah dies in battle, David waits several months before taking Bathsheba as his wife. All seems well until the prophet Nathan shows up one night at the palace. This is the "busted" part we need to reflect on. The prophet Nathan asks David a question through telling a story. We can read this in 2 Samuel Chapter 12.

Nathan tells David about a rich man and a poor man. The rich man had everything in plenty, but the poor man had one little lamb that he cherished. This lamb ate at his table and was part of the family. One day the rich man took the poor man's *only* lamb. He wanted to kill and prepare it as a feast for a guest rather than use one of his own lambs, which he had plenty of. When David heard this story, he said that the rich man deserved to die. Then Nathan gets straight to the hard truth and tells King David that *he* is that man. Nathan goes on to say that God had given David every rich thing He could provide him and more. Can we even imagine the range of emotions that David was feeling right then?

> "Why have you despised the word of the Lord by doing evil in His sight? You have struck down Uriah the Hittite with the sword, have taken his wife to be your wife, and have killed him with the sword of the sons of Ammon. Now therefore, the sword shall never depart from your house, because you have despised Me and have taken the wife of Uriah the Hittite to be your wife" (2 Samuel 12:9-10).

Shortly after, David and Bathsheba lost their child to illness. Every consequence the Lord laid out for them happened, and for the rest of David's earthly life he lived with deep regret of his actions. We read about these times of regret in the Psalms. When you read Psalm chapter 51, you get the image of a broken man who wants to be restored to God. David wrote this psalm right after being confronted by Nathan.

> "Create in me a clean heart, O God, and renew a steadfast spirit within me. Do not cast me away from Your presence and do not take Your Holy Spirit from me. Restore to me the joy of Your salvation and sustain me with a willing spirit" (Psalm 51:10-12).

Avoiding Sin

In spite of all this, the Lord forgave David and blessed him. David was a man of great worship, who had a passionate walk with God. This story not only shows us how we can fall, but reveals the grace of God and His enduring love. Satan likes to divide, but God likes to repair. So what can we do to help us avoid sin? Let's leave with three things.

First, ask God for help. We may not be tempted with certain things, but other temptations rule our life. We need God's help, the cleansing blood of Christ, and true perseverance. We need to ask God to reveal our weaknesses and to walk with us in them. He will join us in those areas and help to lift us up from the hand of the enemy. "Helpless" is a great place to be in our walk with God. Once we are at that point, God can go to work. With God's help we can push back Satan.

Second, we need to surround ourselves with good friends; friends that not only encourage us in our walk with Jesus, but are brave enough to hold us accountable. David had a lot of men in his life to support him. We are not strong enough to do this alone. In Proverbs 27:17 (NLT) it says, "As iron sharpens iron, so a friend sharpens a friend." If we stop and take inventory of our main friend group, is it the best group for us? As a Christian we want to love everyone and invest in their lives, but we need to be strong enough to not allow their choices to affect our walk. When making a decision we should first ask God what He wants us to do rather than looking at which choice our friends are making.

> **If we can stop ourselves from acting when we are in the thought stage, we would save ourselves a lot of trouble.**

Third, guard your thought life. The Word says that our thoughts can become obsessions, and then actions. If we can stop ourselves from acting when we are in the thought stage, we would save ourselves a lot of trouble. The more we know the Word of God, the more He can help us guard our thoughts. His Word and His wisdom somehow begin to rearrange our thinking. The more we learn about Him, the more we strive to be like Him. Reading the Bible regularly will breed smart choices and plant seeds in our minds that will develop into fruit for others, and blessings for our everyday life.

THE TIME TO TESTIFY

"For it is from within, out of a person's heart, that evil thoughts come—sexual immorality, theft, murder, adultery, greed, malice, deceit, lewdness, envy, slander, arrogance and folly" (Mark 7:21-22 NIV).

"Guard your heart above all else, for it determines the course of your life." (Proverbs 4:23 NLT).

I do not want anyone to go into battle without a plan. There have been times I sensed that one of my children were not aware they were even in the battle arena, and I could see they were being led by the enemy with a knife to their back. Whatever temptation they were looking at looked like the answer to their happiness. I have believed the same lies, and I bare scars on my soul from Satan's knife. I don't want that for anyone. Satan's minions are not that smart, but they have had time to study mankind. We are actually quite predictable. Let's take some time today and ask God to evaluate our heart. We need to bring our strongholds to the light and ask for mercy and help from the only source that can bring it quickly. Together we can cry out in the powerful name of Jesus and live in the victory that only He provides.

Meet Anthony Clarke
Freshman at St. John's University
Collegeville, Minnesota

Coming into college, I felt as if I knew exactly who I was in Christ, and I was ready to take on any type of challenge that came my way. But once my mom left and I realized I was no longer surrounded by my community of strong believers, things became extremely difficult. Being away from home, feeling alone, and having zero background knowledge of the people I was going to do life with was a little overwhelming. Something I found extremely helpful in the first couple weeks was knowing that Jesus is constant. He remains the same even when my life felt like a complete disaster, and when I worried that I could not control myself. I learned that He can help me with my messy life, and I did not need to fight alone. It felt great to lean on Him. I am so grateful that He has won the battle for me already, and that when I make a mistake He is not going to leave me stranded. As I began to give my troubles and struggles to Jesus, He gave me mercy and love in return. He did not just leave me hanging with my struggles, but kept giving. *I found as I give to Him, He gives to me.* I find comfort knowing that He is the only one that can beautifully destroy me, and even more beautifully recreate me. He is willing to break any chain, we just need to be willing to give them to Him. Understanding how gracious He is, only motivates me more to be obedient. Let's serve the Lord, not temptation.

Meet Allison Jahn
Recent graduate of the University of Nebraska
Lincoln, Nebraska

Sometimes I think the best image of us and God is portrayed by parents and their children. Children do not always understand what is good for them. If you let a two-year-old roam, they would eat everything in sight (including poison if it is left out). They would somehow manage to stick their fingers in the light sockets, and may fall down a flight of stairs. Thank goodness parents watch out for their children and try to prevent these things from happening. In this world, we are sometimes like two-year-olds. Worse yet, the enemy of our souls does not make these dangers hard to find, but he sticks them right in front of us and tells us how fun it would be to stick our fingers in the light sockets, chew on the electrical wires, and drink the poison. Similar to how children do not understand that these things are harmful, we don't see sin as dangerous because we believe Satan's lies. Sin seems fine, fun even. God tells us to *run* from temptation, and we need to believe that He tells us these things for our good; that His goal is to bring us life and protect us from the damage of sin. Can we trust what He says?

Chapter 7: A Time of Rebellion—Practicing Obedience

*Even though they may be paired against each other,
gladiators in the same school became true comrades.
Many of them pooled a portion of their fight income
so that a fallen gladiator's grieving family could
receive some inheritance, or so a gladiator could have a
deserving burial.*

We are definitely stronger for battle than when we started this process, so let's look at obedience next. This is a place where our best efforts can fail, but God knows we are human, and with His help we can grow in obedience to Him. Of course, God is not asking for perfection, but with His help we should have progress. God is always focused on the heart.

Obedience Brings Blessing

Right now our country is in desperate need for people to honor God and raise His ways above everything else. Our campuses need God's perspective more than ever. This takes courage, integrity, and pure dedication to our Commander and King. If all of us seek a life of obedience towards God, the outcome will be a blessing. All through Scripture you see this truth about God's character. Like clouds about to burst with rain, God is always ready to pour out grace and goodness to the pure hearts that are following His ways.

> "Look, today I am giving you the choice between a blessing and a curse! You will be blessed if you obey the commands of the LORD YOUR GOD THAT I AM GIVING YOU TODAY" (Deuteronomy 11:26-27 NLT).

When I was younger, I remember someone saying they could learn a lot about anyone by looking through their checkbook. Nowadays, it would be more relevant to look at someone's schedule to learn more about them. We can all be invested in many different good things, but sometimes we get too invested in too many things. Our relationship with God often ends at the end of a to-do list, and we find ourselves exhausted and worn. At this point, many of us feel God is being demanding, and His wishes seem like a boatload of work.

In some seasons we even find ourselves burdened by a to-do list from the body of Christ. God's burden is never meant to overwhelm us. His yoke is light and He does the heavy lifting (Matthew 11:30). If we are overwhelmed, we are either filling a role someone else should fill, or carrying a burden that is God's.

> **If we are overwhelmed, we are either filling a role someone else should fill, or carrying a burden that is God's.**

When we are exhausted by any schedule, our obedience will suffer. This exhaustion happens especially when we are trying to please religion rather than God. Religion is something Jesus could not stand.

Not Just Following Rules

Religion is a spiritual counterfeit of the Holy Spirit. At face value, when you hear what religion can offer you it sounds good. Following rules can only make your life better, right? You can look at religious people and feel there consistent life looks pleasant and find them commendable. But this is one of the trapdoors we all need to watch for. God gave us clear commands for how we should live so that our lives bring honor to Him and help us have a blessed life. These commandments, however, were not meant to be worshipped. We do not become more or less worthy based on rules, especially man-made ones.

Religion gives you a list of to-do's and inevitably the list gets longer and longer. It often causes people to start worshipping other people, making God merely a guest in the room, not the King. It is one of Satan's most useful lies, and every time we bow to it, we place weights on our soul. Living out of a list will never bring fruit, only death. In Galatians, Paul warns us to not get caught up in rules.

> "I am emphatic about this. The moment any one of you submits to circumcision or any other rule-keeping system, at that same moment Christ's hard-won gift of freedom is squandered. I repeat my warning: The person who accepts the ways of circumcision trades all the advantages of the free life in Christ for the obligations of the slave life of the law.
>
> "I suspect you would never intend this, but this is what happens. When you attempt to live by your own religious plans and projects, you are cut off from Christ, you fall out of grace. Meanwhile we expectantly wait for a satisfying relationship with the Spirit. For in Christ, neither our most conscientious religion nor disregard of religion amounts to anything. What matters is something far more interior: faith expressed in love" (Galatians 5:2-6 MSG).

Living from a list will become either a burden or a badge. It is choosing slavery over freedom, and is used to damage and separate the body of Christ. Many of us have been saddled with the rules of a dry Christianity, and we crave more of Jesus. Those who live from a list often become self-righteous, or even worse, a huge stumbling block for the unsaved. This bowing to religion breeds hypocrites, and the prideful and idolatrous people who Jesus reprimanded. Jesus wants us to live by the Spirit, not a list. When we live by the Spirit, it breeds life for ourselves and those around us.

People who live by the Spirit live in the freedom of God's grace and exhibit a genuine, simple faith. By allowing themselves to be directed by the Holy Spirit, they begin to walk in gratitude and humility and cast God's love and grace on everyone they encounter. This is the goal of a disciple of Christ and a good ambassador of Jesus. If we are to heal the body of Christ, we need to avoid religion and lean on the Spirit of truth for guidance.

So when we study obedience, we are not talking about rules. Pure obedience is a state of the heart. Jesus fulfilled the law to bring us freedom, yet He was still obedient to His Father. You know you are living by the Spirit if your obedience brings glory to God and not to yourself. We will fail at times and focus on rules, and be judgmental to those around us. This can be hard to avoid. But let's try to discuss obedience to God in its purest form.

What Does Obedience Look Like?

Let's start with the reason we need rest. We know that when we deny our physical body of rest, it does not end well. We get exhausted and everyone around us feels like a burden. Our spiritual bodies need rest too. As a Christian, our obedience can suffer when we are tired. Jesus may be pleased with all that we do in the Spirit, but He still wants us to rest with Him. He wants to spend time with us, and He loves when we spend time before His throne. Walking with Jesus and allowing Him to speak into our lives is imperative for us to thrive. This can be difficult because our culture is such a distraction, and it can take us quite a while to even get into a state where we can hear His voice. Spending time with the King will bring the truest kind of obedience to our lives. How else can we be clear about the direction God has for us if we don't spend time with Him? Even Jesus got away from the crowd to rest, be refilled, and receive direction from God.

A TIME OF REBELLION—PRACTICING OBEDIENCE

This happened after the story of Jesus feeding the five thousand (John 6). This is a familiar miracle story, and we all love it, but let's focus on what happened the next day. The most sobering thing happened the morning after the miracle, and it says a lot about human nature in general. The morning following the miracle, the people Jesus fed began searching for Him. They even got into boats and crossed the sea. When they found Him, He said the most insightful thing.

> "Jesus replied 'The truth of the matter is that you want to be with me because I fed you, not because you believe in me'" (John 6:26 TLB).

Or in my words: "You aren't searching for me because of who I am, but for what I can do for you?" Which begs the question, *do we love Jesus for who He is, or just for what He does for us?*

Do we love Jesus for who He is, or just for what He does for us?

This is a heart-stopping thought. Out of this question, recently our freshman girls and I were doing a study we titled, "Crush on Jesus." Our goal was to make sure that we are getting to know who Jesus is apart from what He does for us.

Let's focus on how Jesus amazingly exemplified obedience to His Father. Many times in the Bible, Jesus says that He is here to do the will of His father (John 6:38); He was not interested in the accolades or acceptance of mere men, or in the treasures of this world. Instead, He was purely focused and desired nothing less than the will of God. Ben Stuart of Breakaway Ministries describes Jesus as a lone soldier parachuting down to our dark world. The crazy part is this soldier's plane took off from there. He had no "back-up" on earth, just his orders from God for the mission to save our souls.

In a nutshell, *obedience* is sometimes setting aside what we want to do and doing things another person's way. This can be tough. But it normally gets easier for us to be obedient when we can see immediate results. What if we could find a pair of glasses that allowed us to see the benefits of reverence to God? We know there are rewards when we are obedient to God that far out measure anything we can see with our eyes. It is still good to push ourselves in many areas of our life, but let's discuss the spiritual "muscle" of this commitment to God and see if we want to start flexing it.

The book of Deuteronomy is basically a book of God's expectations for the nation of Israel. It goes over many rules that show God's desire for reverence in most every facet of their lives. We know that Jesus came and ultimately fulfilled the laws of Moses (Matthew 5:17), but we still need this background to understand God's true yearning for dedicated hearts.

> "And you shall do what is right and good in the sight of the Lord, that it may be well with you" (Deuteronomy 6:18a).

> "Now it shall be, if you diligently obey the Lord your God, being careful to do all His commandments which I command you today, the Lord your God will set you high above all the nations of the earth" (Deuteronomy 28:1).

When we are obedient, it is guaranteed that it comes with blessings for this life. When Adam sinned in the Garden of Eden he had immediate and long-term consequences for that decision. We are still bearing the consequences of Adam's mistake today. In the book of Roman's it says that from Adam we are cursed, but from Jesus we are blessed.

Satan knows how to pull our strings, and he tricked Adam and Eve. If only Adam and Eve would have taken a second to run their idea by God. We alone have to give an account of our lives on earth. When we minimize our sin it may appease our flesh, but it does not appease God. Obedience to God is a marathon that is impossible to get perfect, but we must give it our all.

Jesus had perfect obedience. He is a model of acquiescence that we can all aspire too. We will never be perfect, but with God's help we should have progress in our toughest areas. The Bible tells us that if we acknowledge God in all our ways, He will make our paths straight (Proverbs 3:5). We need to count on Him for this promise. He is not expecting anything from us that He will not help us attain.

One perfect example of reverence to God came in the garden of Gethsemane. It is overwhelming to realize that Jesus knew what was coming; He knew that He would be arrested and ultimately fulfill God's call as the sacrifice for all of humanity. Because Jesus was the Son of Man and the Son of God, His humanity knew that this would be painful beyond measure and brutal to suffer through, but His godliness knew that this was the ultimate goal of His mission on earth and He would be home in heaven soon.

It is sad, yet comforting because this picture of His human suffering is one we can draw on when we are suffering. We will all have a Gethsemane moment in our lifetime that is much the same. There will be a time where we feel alone, misunderstood, and powerless to avoid an oncoming trial.

There will be a time where we feel alone, misunderstood, and powerless to avoid an oncoming trial.

It can give us amazing strength to know that Jesus, in His humanity, demonstrated what to do at a time like that. Three times in Matthew chapter 26 Jesus says virtually the same thing.

> "And He went a little beyond them, and fell on His face and prayed, saying, 'My Father, if it is possible, let this cup pass from Me; *yet not as I will, but as You will.*'…. He went away again a second time and prayed, saying, 'My Father, if this cannot pass away unless I drink it, *Your will be done.*'…and He left them again, and went away and prayed a third time, saying the same thing once more" (Matthew 26:39, 42, 44, emphasis mine).

We can kneel in our Gethsemane moments, telling God that we do not want this trial and we would like Him to please take it away, joining

Jesus in this prayer: "Please, God, take this cup from me. This cup of sickness, worry, divorcing parents, finals, anorexia, addiction, self-hatred, or (fill in the blank with your own present trial), is not a cup I ever wanted. Please take this from me, I did not know I was signing up for this."

The next part of Jesus' prayer is ultimately the perfect picture of obedience to a sovereign God. "Not My will, but Yours be done!" Jesus turned His will over to God from the moment He drew a breath. He lived His life in flawless obedience. He was not even slightly distracted by anything outside His purpose to serve His Father. He was laser-focused on saving our souls, and He perfectly demonstrated a fierce love of God and a mammoth heart for mankind.

My Gethsemane Moment

My Gethsemane moment came when my son Jack was four years old. He was such a great kid. Our daughter Brooke was two at this time. My world was so full and blessed. We lived in a little house a few miles from my husband's insurance office, and life was glorious. (You don't understand how children steal your heart until you hold your own. It is love beyond measure!)

One day, Jack started to follow me around and he was sort of mumbling. I stopped what I was doing and tried to understand what he was saying and I realized that he couldn't speak. I gave him a ball and he could not even hold the ball in his hand. This was alarming because Jack could throw a ball in the air and hit it with his own bat at seventeen months of age. He played with balls and hockey sticks all day. I knew there was something terribly wrong, so I raced him to the clinic.

They assessed him and called the ambulance. I remember like it was yesterday. The medic in the ambulance asked me if this was my only son, and it was like he put a whale harpoon through my chest. I couldn't imagine why he would have asked me that. I was delirious with worry as Jack was deteriorating right before my eyes. I remember seeing Mark through the window in the back of the ambulance as he was driving our car behind us. His face was like a ghost. Somehow we knew that our world would never be the same.

It turns out that Jack had suffered a stroke. The neurologist at the children's hospital called every neurologist he could between Minnesota and Florida and could not find one that had dealt with this. It was rare to have a stroke under the age of fifty, and Jack was only four. I cried out like never before, "Please take this cup from me!"

As the days turned into a week, Jack was deteriorating even more. He had not spoken since the event took place and could not walk. I remember asking a play therapist if he ever will talk again, and she honestly told me that the doctors did not know. I could tell he was getting worse, and he was hardly supporting his own weight. I alerted the doctors to this, and they did another scan of his brain. They told us that he was probably about to have another stroke and this time it would affect a lot of brain. They could either let that happen and he would lose more function, or they could try a drug that was rarely used in children and could cause him to die.

Mark and I decided to believe for the best and try the drug, and they administered it to him that evening. I can still remember the fear I felt at two o'clock that morning. The bone-rattling anxiety was unimaginable. At one point I asked the nurses if someone could please come cut his hair, I wanted him to look handsome for his funeral. I was almost certain at times that we were losing him, and then I would tell myself to get a grip and enjoy the fact I could hold his hand and watch him sleep.

At about three in the morning I remember praying and looking out of the hospital window. I said to God, "It's okay, if You need him in heaven You can take him." I cried my eyes out and gave Jack over to God's care. It sounds funny, but I asked that if He took my "Jacko," He would be there to hold him and show him around until he was not afraid. To this day, when I think about that night I am overwhelmed with emotion.

I guess I realized that this situation was a "God thing," and we needed God to show us what was best for Jack. I knew he needed care that we could not give him on earth. This was my Gethsemane moment, I joined Jesus in praying, "Not my will, but yours be done." This does not mean that I would have grieved Jack without terrible pain and anger if He took him, nor was it a moment where I feel like God changed His plan. At about four in the morning the neurologist came in and sat with me. He said that his wife told him he better come check on Jack because she knew he was not going to sleep. We just sat in silence and waited until morning.

Miraculously, God saved Jack that night! Four days later he was taking his first steps and starting to talk again. But Jack could have died; I don't know if my prayer changed the outcome, but praying brought me peace that I cannot explain.

Currently, Jack is a senior at the University of Minnesota, Duluth. He is a walking miracle. I still remember how he would kick his left leg out a little extra when he was relearning to walk, and it seemed that soon after he was back on his hockey skates, moving as fast as ever. He enjoyed this Minnesota tradition with perseverance of a kind I have never witnessed all throughout his high school years. We were told many things that scared us about Jack's future, but thankfully God had much different plans.

Let's read and pray about Jesus's words on our obedience to Him.

> "*If you love me*, you will keep my commandments" (John 14:15, emphasis mine).

> "He who has My commandments and keeps them *is the one who loves Me*; and he who loves Me will be loved by My Father, and I will love him and will disclose Myself to him" (John 14:21, emphasis mine).

A couple thoughts:

- Lets keep our focus. Make sure God is calling us to do something, and then do it.

- Let's ask God to use our day, rather than bless our day.

- Let's join God in His work on earth instead of asking Him to join ours.

The disciple Peter is a great person to study. Jesus' first words to Peter were "follow Me," and interestingly, Jesus' last words to Peter were also "follow me." In between those two commands, Peter's walk with Jesus was not always perfect but Jesus still said He wanted to build His church through Peter. Jesus saw Peter's intentions. God loves an earnest heart. It is always about the heart. Let's seek good, spread God's love and mercy, and follow Jesus at every turn.

> **Peter's walk with Jesus was not always perfect but Jesus still said He wanted to build His church through Peter.**

Meet Sarah Watne
Sophomore at Colorado Christian University
Lakewood, Colorado

When did obedience become an ugly thing? We hear the word and almost cringe. We think of merely fulfilling obligatory duties, doing stuff because we have to and not because we have an all-consuming desire fueled by *love*. Jesus said the most important commandment is to "Love the Lord your God with all your heart, and with all your soul, and with all your mind, and with all your strength" (Mark 12:28-30). What if we redefined obeying God to simply loving Him? God is beckoning us in. He is constantly and earnestly asking us to just love on Him and to just *be with Him*. Obedience is not merely the discipline of observing God's commands. Discipline might keep us in obedience for a while, but it alone can't be what propels us. A revelation of our Father's love for us can fuel our obedience, and keep us in hot pursuit of Him. Obedience is loving Him, coming to Him, abiding in Him, and dwelling with Him.

When we do these things, we find love. Obedience doesn't bind us up in a boring life, like I once thought. It brings freedom. It allows us to surrender ourselves—our canvases—to the Great Artist who never makes mistakes. It ultimately grants Him permission to gently place His hand on ours to guide every brushstroke of our lives.

Meet Connor Haugen
Junior at Bethel University
St. Paul, Minnesota

My favorite aspect of college so far has been my involvement in the track and cross country programs. Running was something that I enjoyed doing in high school, but during my college years running became my identity.

At the beginning of my junior season of cross country here at Bethel University, I felt God was calling me to give it up. Unfortunately, I ignored it. Why would God call me to give up something that was so important to me? I wasn't willing to listen, and as a result my spiritual life became stagnant during this season.

It all came to a head during fall break of that same year. I was sick of my disobedience and I knew I needed to get my heart right with God. I locked myself in my room and sought the Lord. He led me to read 1 Samuel 15, where Saul disobeys God and the prophet Samuel tells Saul in verse 22 that God doesn't value our sacrifice as much as our obedience. At that point I knew I had to give up running cross country.

I met with my spiritual mentors and they affirmed what God was speaking to me. I was convinced that I needed to do this and put God first in my life. While I was driving home, I began to pray. I asked God, "Well, what now?" And He answered, "Go for a run." Exasperated and confused, I begrudgingly put on my shorts and went for a run. During this particular run, God ministered to my heart and fully revealed His plan. He said that running was constantly fighting with Him for Lordship over my life, and that He had to bring me to the point of giving it up in order for Him to be the Master. It was an Abraham and Isaac sort of exercise: He called me to do something, but then He gave it back to me because of my place on the team, and because of my passion for running.

I am still part of this team that I love, but God is now first-place in my life. If He truly wants me to quit in the future, I can do so with no questions asked. God must be first in our lives if we are to follow Him. Obedience is much more valuable than sacrifice.

Meet Lauren Watne
Sophomore at Colorado Christian University
Lakewood, Colorado

When we think about obedience, we often tend to see it like a list to check off in order to please God. It can be easy to forget that He is already pleased with us and already sees us as righteous. It's true that we don't have to *do* anything to *earn* His approval, which is the exact opposite from the lies that Satan spews. Satan wants us to struggle to get to a place of favor with the Lord until we burn out and give up on following His ways. In reality, we already won God's favor when Jesus died for us.

The core of obedience is a passionate love for Jesus. Without this passion our actions are just good morals and ethics, not worship. Ethics and morals without relationship lead to religion, and soon you will find (and have probably already discovered) that you will burn out when you do things to please the religious. Religion always focuses on what *you do*, not *who God is*.

As you get to know Jesus and understand His heart, the more you will want to follow Him. Somewhere along the way your flesh will die, and your heart will become irrational for one name and one name only— Jesus. All obedience is in vain if it's not birthed out of loving Him. Obedience should always be a response of worship to the King of Kings, never a burden, but rather a sweet response of affection.

Chapter 8: For Times of Doubt—Holding High Your Faith

There were strict rules about which types of gladiators could fight each other. One specialty group was called the Scissores. Not surprisingly, their weapon looked like giant slashing scissors. They were often paired against the Retiarius, whom were net-fighters. Both wore very light armor.

Football is one of my favorite sports to watch, but it is a complex game to understand for a casual fan. It was my son Ryan's favorite sport to play, and his games were a great place for me to learn the sport. One thing that interested me was how each team would share film of their previous games so their opponents could prepare for Friday night. It was a huge part of football strategy to try to predict an opponent's offensive plays and stop them from gaining any yards.

Our military also uses intelligence to gain advantage during war. We have intelligence agents working in places all over the world. The more we know about our enemies the easier it is to gain victory.

We can diligently plan for a football game, and spy on our enemies in wartime, but we often miss this defensive awareness in our spiritual battle here on earth. Our adversary is not actually that smart. When we become more aware of his offensive moves, we can battle him before he gains a foothold in our minds. We can start to discover how we are personally attacked and make a battle plan.

When it comes to faith, Satan has one trick I have recently been made aware of. It is a type of diversion method. He wants us to believe that God considers our past when deciding if He will help us in the future. So our hopes and dreams **Satan wants us to believe that God considers our past when deciding if He will help us in the future.** are knit into our own skewed picture of worthiness, instead of on God's unchanging character. It is like smoke and mirrors. For example, let's say we are trying to get over an addiction and we still crave a substance. We know that on our own strength it will be impossible to heal, and we need a powerful miracle. In this scenario, our enemy may try to get us to focus on our past, telling us that God is not going to come to our aid. He wants us to believe that God has no time for us because of our mistakes. If we begin to doubt our worth to God, we will look at our future with fear. Metaphorically, our adversary has us in a headlock and is twisting our face to only see the past. If we stay in this position we are sure to struggle. Are we going to rest our head in his arms, or are we going to call on Jesus with all we have? Great acts of faith come when we count on God's character and not our own, and we allow God to be God.

> "What is faith? It is the confident assurance that something we want is going to happen. It is the certainty that what we hope for is waiting for us, even though we cannot see it up ahead" (Hebrews 11:1 TLB).

Faith is a verb in some cases. Yes, we have faith in Jesus. But, we also can live by faith, and walk in faith. When someone decides to become a follower of Jesus and lays their life down for Him, they become filled with the Holy Spirit. It is amazing how once the Holy Spirit begins a work in us we begin to see the world differently. We become convicted when we sin, more loving to people around us, less self-focused, and we gain a hunger for the Word of God like never before. Our eyes are opened to the spiritual realm around us, and we begin to see God at work everywhere. Being a new Christian is both amazing and hard at the same time. What is tough is when we know enough about God to give us unending passion, but not enough to answer all of our questions. When it comes to battling with power, we need to know God's true character, and that comes with time. It would be great to have a few hundred years to learn how to do this, but we only get this short time on earth to walk by faith. In heaven we will live by sight and will no longer need a faith in the unseen. We will finally join the angels and see God in all His glory.

It is fascinating for us to consider the difference between us and angels. It is believed that the angels were created along with the heavens in Genesis chapter 1, so they have not been in existence forever, like God has. Many guess that the number of angels in God's army is probably as great as the number of humans that cover the earth. This is amazing to picture. They are in the spiritual realm and are serving God and mankind in the natural realm, to God's great pleasure.

You can find over two hundred references about angels in the Bible, and yet this only gives us a snapshot of their activities through the ages. They were created for a different purpose than us. Angels are different than humans and they do not marry, procreate, or die. When we are in heaven we will not be angels.

The word *angel* in Greek is *aggelos*, which means "messenger." There are instances in the Bible where an angel made an appearance in the flesh and delivered a timely message as they did for Moses. They also brought warnings in dreams to Joseph, and food to Elijah.

It is believed that angels will carry us to heaven when we die, as angels received the spirit of Lazarus as written in Luke. They are true warriors in the heavenly realm, and God is the admiral of them all. They are stronger and smarter than humans, and considered greater than us. We don't think of them often, but they are busy over earth and have fought ruthlessly for our causes, and it is hard for us to fathom how much they have impacted our daily lives.

THE TIME TO TESTIFY

But, as we think about angels and humans there is one thing that should inspire us all. Angels can never live by faith. It is not that we are trying to compete with them, because they will be greater than us in heaven, but the point is that because they can see God they don't need faith. Faith is something mankind was created for. As a human, when we live by faith it brings a special pleasure to God. This should inspire us. When we step out in faith, all of heaven celebrates.

We get this one life to live by faith. Once we are dead, we can't live by faith again. While we can, let's stick our neck out, even when it is scary, and allow God to use us.

We get this one life to live by faith. Once we are dead, we can't live by faith again.

Of course, this is all easier said than done for me. The desire to make the most of my time here on earth came to me a few years back when a friend of mine named Daniel Wickham told me that he has a list in his Bible of everything we can't do in heaven. I had never thought of that. Shortly after discussing this with Daniel, I was reading about how we will all bow down to Jesus when He makes His return here (Romans 14:11). Even though I had read this passage many times, the verse and the amazing scene it depicts took shape in my mind like never before. How amazing to picture the whole world bowing to Jesus!

I decided then that I did not want the first time I bow down to my King to be when I see Him along with the rest of the world. So now I find myself wanting to physically bow before Him occasionally. This may seem like a very small act of faith, and it may not be the way God wants someone else to act in their walk with Him, but it honestly overwhelms me when I do it. I guess I desire that when I am in heaven I will reflect on some seasons in my life where I lived by faith. I know it will never be perfect, and it probably won't make the news, but I want to give it my best anyway. This is not to try and earn favor with God, but simply because I am grateful for Him.

The Amazing Faith of Jordan Davis

As a pediatric/adult oncology nurse I have seen many high school age people discover they have cancer, some of them incurable. I want to write about a patient that I was a primary nurse to that blessed my life.

This patient was named Jordan. She lived with cancer during her junior and senior year of high school like nobody else I had ever witnessed. First, her response to finding out that she had cancer was so accepting. She told me at her first chemo that she figures if someone was to get it, it may as well be her. She wouldn't want anyone else to have it, but thought she was pretty tough. I wish you all could have met Jordan because she was very charismatic. When I picture her steadfast faith and honorable acceptance of this trial, it always amazes me.

When Jordan realized she only had a few months to live she posted a bucket list on her social media accounts. She was just having fun, but miraculously she had many people offer to fulfill some of her wishes. One of her wishes was to be a queen for the day, and a popular festival in our area made that happen. She was literally Queen Jordan for the day. She had attendants and held court here in Minneapolis. It was amazing. She wore a costume so big she even needed help to go to the bathroom. Also, she had a trumpeter announcing her throughout the park everywhere she wandered.

When Jordan turned eighteen she made the choice to stop treatment. Her family struggled a little with that decision but Jordan did not. She told me that she felt like she was ready for heaven. I still feel so blessed to have witnessed her walk with Jesus and her steadfast faith in the midst of a horrible trial. It makes me smile to think of her in heaven, and I can't wait to see her again.

Jordan knew something we need to grasp. We need to understand that this life is not about the rewards of this world. Whoever said we deserve good health and perfect accommodations at all times? Maybe, just maybe, God has plans to use our lives in a bigger way than we ever imagined.

THE TIME TO TESTIFY

Faith: Believing in the Unseen

I need to be honest with you all that living by faith is very hard for me. Because of my abuse as a child I often wonder if Jesus will protect me and if I am worthy to Him at all. I know He is worthy, but am I? I have been wrestling with this for many seasons of my life, but as I have been writing this chapter the Lord has provided me with a key truth I need to share.

He reminded me that we need to look at a challenge through the lens of God's worth and not through our lens of self-worth. God is the same yesterday, today, and tomorrow. He does not change—ever. For us to say that God shows up in other people's lives but not our own is a lie. If it were true that God will provide for everyone else but us, then the Bible is a lie. It is almost reverse pride to get to the point where we feel like we are the one person in all of creation that could cause God to go back on His Word. **It is not humility, but pride. It is making "me" too big of a deal.**

God told me to forget my feelings about any situation and focus on His character. I have started doing this when I am afraid by picturing Him when He suffered on the cross, and then picturing myself below Him on my knees. When I am kneeling below the cross I can fully picture His love for me. If He would gladly die for me, then I know that He also delights in helping me when I am in trouble.

Let's read about one person who obviously knew God's character well, and walked by faith in a society driven by evil desires. Hebrews chapter 11 is referred to as the "Hall of Faith." If this were written today, maybe one of us would be listed in this chapter. Almost every verse tells a story of someone in the Bible who had great faith. In verse 7 it talks about Noah.

100

FOR TIMES OF DOUBT—HOLDING HIGH YOUR FAITH

> "By faith Noah, being warned by God about things *not yet seen*, in reverence prepared an ark for the salvation of his household" (Hebrews 11:7a, emphasis mine).

There are so many great parts to Noah's story, but the writer of Hebrews is talking about Noah's faith. Notice it talks about things Noah had never seen? He had never seen rain, let alone a flood! We can only imagine the taunting and teasing he got from the locals when he was building an ark in the middle of the desert. It is amazing that Noah still continued to warn them and love them as he built the ark.

I have always thought two of the most powerful words in the Bible are, "but Noah." It may sound funny, but at this time God regretted creating humans at all. He was ready to take humankind out and start all over again. *But Noah* pleased God, and we are all blessed because of his life. It gives me pause whenever I read his story in Genesis. It is amazing to think that God could look down and see masses and generations of people, and as His eyes swept through the land they could rest on one person and be pleased.

At times we all may receive taunting and teasing about our walk with God like Noah. I remember my daughter Brooke being teased about her faith. She went through some tough high school years because she did not want to forsake her promises to God to live under His authority. But she was steadfast and now she is in college surrounded by many good friends. Her mourning has turned into dancing. One of her favorite verses in the Bible gave her hope through the persecution.

> "Blessed are you when people insult you and persecute you, and falsely say all kinds of evil against you because of Me. Rejoice and be glad, for your reward in heaven is great; for in the same way they persecuted the prophets who were before you" (Matthew 5:11-12).

THE TIME TO TESTIFY

When we feel alone, we need to know that we are suffering the same fate as many who came before us. Jesus understands what it is like to be persecuted. Even His own family and town ridiculed Him.

My final words on faith are something my cabin girls and I ran into at camp. One student named Laurel asked me to tell them all I know about the prophet Malachi. I decided we needed to read that book. We were absolutely taken aback by a portion of Malachi that we studied. It is an important portion of Scripture that we all need to review, and apply to our life.

The end of Chapter 3 talks about a group of people who were sick of following God and felt there was no blessing in it. They were tired of seeing the lawless people around them be blessed when they themselves faced hardship. We have all felt that way at times and wondered how some who even proclaim to worship Satan can live an outwardly successful life.

These people wondered out loud how it profits them to follow God. How come people who live evil lives seem to flourish? They felt like the wicked people were not being punished by God, some even appeared to be blessed, and they were confused. This is still true today, there are always people who by their own words are far from God, yet they appear to have it all together. But what we need to realize is that God is doing things in our lives that will bring us much more blessing than any earthly treasure.

> **God is doing things in our lives that will bring us much more blessing than any earthly treasure.**

The next portion of Scripture in Malachi gave the girls and I the chills as we read it. It talks about a few that were faithful at this time. Imagine this being any of us. We need this reminder that heaven is watching!

"Then those who feared the Lord spoke to one another, and the *Lord gave attention and heard it,* and a book of remembrance was written before Him for those who fear the Lord and who esteem His name. 'They will be mine,' says the Lord of hosts, 'on the day that I prepare My own possession, and I will spare them as a man spares his own son who serves him.' So you will again distinguish between the righteous and the wicked, between one who serves God and one who does not serve Him" (Malachi 3:16-18, emphasis mine).

This part made our group so excited that we were screaming! What if *our* names were written down on one of these scrolls? Just the thought that the Lord could give us His attention when we take a stand in faith is so exciting.

God is not asking us to build an Ark. Although you never know what is coming. No act of faith is a small thing. People around us are watching, and even if they may occasionally chuckle at us, they still will recognize that we are in a safe place with Jesus. They will see the peace in our hearts and the love in our actions. Then when their life becomes a flood-fest, they will know where to run. Let's have our ark ready and waiting!

Meet Nate Schaefer
Senior in Robotics at Hennepin Technical Program
Minneapolis, MN

Living by faith never meant much to me until I started to have a relationship with God. Before this relationship I only had faith that God was real and that the Bible was truth. But my new oneness with God started to bring both God and the Bible alive to the point where God became my Father and the Bible became His voice. With that established, I realized that He wasn't only telling His story, but also preparing mine. Every time He speaks, He is building my identity—things that I don't see in myself, He is calling out. He is not only showing me who I am but what I am capable of doing through Him. Living by faith is necessary for me, because even if I can't see His definition of who I am and my actions often contradict the character He is developing in me, faith holds me to the truth of my identity in Him. God continues to stretch me and I feel the need to be more reliant on my Father's ability working through me instead of on my own strength. My relationship with Him was the key to my breakthrough because I know that I can always trust Him to build me up, steer me in the right direction, and give me a pep talk when I need it. Things often end different than I would expect, but *He has never failed me*. He has remained faithful, so I am inspired to pray and keep the passion in our relationship by listening, believing, obeying, and acting in faith, knowing He is for me and never against me. It is my desire that my life is lived for His glory!

Meet Brooke Ylitalo
Senior at Bethel University
St. Paul, Minnesota

Many people talk about how they want their life to be an adventure. They want to "live on the edge" and avoid the common life. Adventure is not usually defined as an event that went exactly as planned. Instead it often is an event that *did not go* as planned, and left people flying by the seat of their pants. I am starting to learn that life with God is like this kind of adventure. It is not a well-planned out itinerary; it often requires risks. We are often asked to take steps of faith, even when it is into the unknown. Sometimes we need to take a step in the opposite direction of our desires or even into our deepest fears. Occasionally, it may feel like a step off of a cliff, or more particularly, a shove onto a plane heading to a foreign country for a summer of the unknown.

This past summer I did just that. The Lord was very persistent in telling me to go to the Philippines to serve His people. It took a lot of convincing on His part, but eventually I listened. I took that first step and said yes. Over the next few weeks following that decision, Satan threw every insecurity, worry, and doubt in the book at me. He showered me with questions and concerns, and tried so desperately to get me to turn around and not go on the trip. But the Lord was persistent, and I kept taking those small steps of faith through my doubt.

About three weeks into my trip was when I started to struggle with culture shock and I was very homesick. I felt like I was at the end of myself, and had nothing left to give these beautiful people. It was during this week that faith in God's plan for me was the only thing I could hold onto. I didn't have my family, I didn't have my friends, I didn't even have Chipotle (lame, I know). God was my only familiarity. He was all I had to draw on, and He showed up bigtime.

In the Philippines I took many bucket showers. I got used to them eventually and they were okay because they basically accomplished my mission, to get clean. But I was still never quite satisfied; I missed my normal shower at home.

As I was struggling with the culture shock and missing home, I found that once I was able to push through my hard week and give up my independence, it was like Jesus spiritually replaced my bucket showers with an ocean. He brought the refreshing my spirit needed. His grace no longer came in small amounts that I could easily handle, but in overwhelming amounts that I had no idea what to do with. Once I allowed Him to, He poured out His love in measures that felt undeserving. What I came to realize was that Jesus had been offering me the ocean the whole time, I just sheepishly picked the bucket shower because I was scared there might be some sort of catch. I had to step out in faith to receive the wellspring that Jesus had been offering me. Boy can I tell you, it was well worth it! I would do it all again in a heartbeat to receive the ocean that Jesus has blessed me with, and the abundance I found when I replaced doubt with faith.

Meet Andrea Polis
Sophomore at University of Wisconsin Madison
Madison, Wisconsin

Going to a Big Ten school excited me, but also held a touch of fear; mainly because I worried that my faith would be stifled by the college party scene that seemed to constantly surround me. As a freshman, I felt ready for the battle; with God at my side I can conquer anything right? Yes, this is true, but my problem was that I viewed God as another one of my soldiers, not my commander in chief. I thought of Him when

I felt like I needed Him, but He wasn't an ever-present force in my life. It's hard to surrender your life to a God you may be unsure of. When you walk in faith, however, you walk in assurance that no matter where life takes you, the Creator of the universe is looking out for you. Jeremiah 29:11 tells us that God has a plan for your life and wants to see it through every step of the way. This was a hard lesson for me to learn, and it certainly hasn't stopped me from making mistakes.

After a year of doing it my way, I finally threw up my hands and truly surrendered my life to pursue Jesus, and a lot changed. I broke up with the boyfriend who I thought was leading me towards God but really wasn't. I quit the sorority that I felt like I was forcing myself into. The biggest change was that I finally found a new confidence in my beliefs outside of what I had learned in Sunday school. I could feel the love of Christ welling up inside of me and began to live day by day with an inner peace that I didn't know was possible. None of this would have happened had I not made the conscious decision to walk by faith. I gave up a lot of things that I thought were making me happy and weren't, and instantly felt relief. God showed me the best life ever when I fell to my knees. Surrendering all you are and all you have to walk by faith is ultimately the only decision that's going to bring lasting peace and happiness.

> "Trust in the Lord with all your heart and do not lean on your own understanding. In all your ways acknowledge Him and He will make your paths straight" (Proverbs 3:5-6).

Chapter 9: Time for the Warrior Pose—The Fierceness of Love

It is believed that two famous gladiators named Priscus and Verus fought for so long that the emperor declared a draw when they both conceited defeat at the same moment. Amazingly, they were both awarded a Rudis, and walked out the Gate of Life together.

A s I have been writing this book, I have been praying that our lanista would help us all discover our inner gladiator. I found myself gritting my teeth as I pictured the Colosseum, the roaring crowd, and our crafty adversary with a smirk on his face. But as I wrote the chapter about shame, I realized something profound. It came to me like a light bulb moment, and I knew it was wisdom from the Lord.

I realized that if we miss the extent of how much God loves us, we *can't* love the world like He desires, nor be a respectable ambassador. God revealed to me that by realizing how much He loves me, I can spread that same love to others. He told me that love is the greatest weapon of all. The strongest warriors for God, the gladiators that really kick it, are those that know how to love. Love wins every time! There is no power in hell or in humanity that can overpower love. The Bible says three powerful words about love. *Love never fails.* This changes everything; it turns our whole world upsidedown! Love can propel us forward in warrior fashion.

THE TIME TO TESTIFY

From an earthly perspective love can seem wimpy. Turning the other cheek and giving people another chance will not always feel victorious. But the greatest evidence for love's power is that Jesus—out of love—died on the cross and defeated hell. Satan and his army had to be screaming when they realized that Jesus' death opened the door for our bleeding hearts and gave us eternal refuge from his gang of thugs. If hell was defeated out of an act of love, then we know its power is endless.

> **If hell was defeated out of an act of love, then we know its power is endless.**

God was holding out the big kahuna from us until this chapter. The reason this book was started was out of love, and the finishing theme is a call to love. In God's great fashion, everything comes full circle.

If we want to change the world, if we have dreamed of making an impact, if we want to battle Satan, then let's choose love. Learning to love like Jesus will never fail us. It will open up endless opportunities for God to bring transformation to our world. We will be part of God's Special Forces team, and become the warriors that we never knew existed.

We have heard so many cute quips surrounding the word *love*. Greeting card companies have made millions off of the word, and in our own lives it has been cheaply passed around. Let's discover something new about love. We already talked about loving ourselves, but how can we increase in love for those around us? Our lanista is talking about working toward pure love. Loving everyone at all times and with all we have. This is a tall task without God's help, but worth our effort. Let's look at one definition of *love* from the Word.

> "Love is patient, love is kind. It does not envy, it does not boast, it is not proud. It does not dishonor others, it is not self-seeking, it is not easily angered, it keeps no record of wrongs. Love does not delight in evil but rejoices with the truth. It always protects, always

trusts, always hopes, always perseveres. Love never fails" (1 Corinthians 13:4-8 NIV).

You won't find this definition of *love* in the dictionary. Most explanations we read elsewhere focus on a feeling. These are not feelings, but actions. Love is not for feeble people. Love is a show of strength that takes heaven's power to pull off. This chapter is not for the faint of heart. But God, in His grace, demonstrated His love so we would know how to pursue this important call on our lives.

The word *sacrifice* is not listed in the verses in 1 Corinthians highlighted above, but is implied in every part of that passage. Sacrifice is the glue that holds those words together. Every part of our call to love starts with less self-focus, and plenty of heart for mankind. Sacrificial love is the hardest love to give and it is no surprise that it brings the greatest pleasure to God.

My daughter Brooke interned last summer in the Philippines at a birthing home. The birthing home was started by a missionary named Mavis who saw a desperate need in the community she was serving. Mavis did not head to the Philippines to fill this need, but heard the voice of God calling her to this country. When she arrived, she would walk through the villages and see caskets much more frequently than she would suspect. When she would ask family members about who the casket was for, she would be informed that most were filled with mothers who had died in childbirth. Having a background in midwifery, she opened her home and spread the news that she would deliver babies. The first month she delivered eight babies in her living room; within a few months she was delivering an average of 120 babies a month. What a sacrifice!

When we adopted Katie it was a learning experience. She was nine years old. She had lived her first four years in a tough situation in Delhi, spent time on the street as a runaway, and three years in an orphanage before coming to America. We went into it quite naïve, not realizing it would take a good six years before she felt at home with us. This decision was clearly God's call on our family, but came with sacrifice for Katie and all of us.

We all learned a lot about God's love for us by working together. It was humbling to realize He adores us, though we often question our place in His family. He loves us even when we do not want His love. Luckily, His constant love eventually wins us over and helps us feel safe. That is the love we had to learn to give to Katie to make this work for her.

On a particularly hard day I learned of a family so sacrificial that I can't even find the words to describe it.

I was at my son Brad's basketball tournament and I met a girl that looked like Katie at the concession stand. I saw her call a white girl "sister," and I became intrigued. I had to know if they were truly from the same family and similar to ours. So I decided to ask her about her family. I was taken back when I heard her response. She explained that she was one of ten adopted children in a large family close by. Her mom and dad had adopted children from all over the world, and were planning a trip at the time to adopt an eight-year-old from Russia with HIV. This family did not just adopt children, but sought to adopt the children that were not easy to place in families. They have children with all kinds of disabilities and health issues, and they are one huge loving family. This is the picture I see when I think about how God wants us to love others. If we could love like that family loves, this world would be so different.

We often have trouble sharing even the most basic items, much less our home. We may be generous with our money or our time, but are we sacrificial? God is the giver of all good things, and everything that we have essentially belongs to God. We complain about the state of the world, and forget to take accountability. When the world stinks, it is because the meat is rotting, and we have the salt it needs. We are called to be the salt and light for the world that God loves so much (Matthew 5). We have to begin to see others the way Jesus did and give love in abundance.

TIME FOR THE WARRIOR POSE—THE FIERCENESS OF LOVE

Let's walk together through a bit of Scripture and try to wrap our minds around what Jesus wants. What does Jesus say about love? Jesus says the greatest commandment is to love God with all our heart, and love our neighbor like ourselves (Matthew 22:37-40). Even if we only lived out one verse, this one would keep us busy our whole earthly life.

Let's decide to be a messenger and example of His love to everyone we meet. He is calling us to love the depressed person, the gothic person, and the person who seems too perfect. He is calling us to love the lady with the funny laugh, the guy who corrects our English, the person who quotes Scripture, and the people who play their music too loud. He is calling us to love that person who we have hated under our breath, the addict, the junkie, the preppy boy, and the athlete. Each is deserving of our love, if God finds all deserving.

I looked up the family with the ten adopted kids online and, and it was no surprise to find out that they are Christians. Are they millionaires? No. Their daughter told me they save funds diligently for each child they can add to their family. When they travel, they make peanut butter and jelly sandwiches to save money. There is a saying on their website that is profound:

> "Sometimes I would like to ask God why He allows
> poverty, famine and injustice in the world when He
> could do something about it….But I am afraid He is
> going to ask me the same question."
> -Anonymous

Clearly, this family lives this statement out every day. I emailed the mother recently to see if I could mention their family in this chapter. She informed me that they were leaving in one month to get a beautiful new eight-year-old daughter from China. What a wonderful example of what Jesus wants from all of us! What are we going to do about that call on our own lives?

THE TIME TO TESTIFY

Love One Another

> "A new command I give you: Love one another. As I have loved you, so you must love one another. By this everyone will know you are my disciples, if you love one another" (John 13:34-35 NIV).

Telling people that we are His disciple is not enough, but people will *know* we are His disciple *if* we love one another. This is a challenge for every generation and it is sitting before us now. It is the biggest challenge of our time, and it is imperative that we try to get this right.

The number one problem we are facing as Christians today is that we are being labeled as judgmental. This is a huge affront that is eagerly spread through social media. This also comes because many Christians have been judgmental, and it is our consequence as a body to fix this.

Not only are we judging people that do not follow Christ, we are judging each other.

Not only are we judging people that do not follow Christ, we are judging each other.

My husband and I have had many conversations about judgment. We have been judged by many people we love because of our walk with Christ. But we were wondering if judging is ever a correct thing to do? We have come to the conclusion that the best time to use judgment is when we are judging darkness and light in our own lives, and comparing a teaching to the Word of God. We need to be a lover of the truth and able to judge God's way for our own heart and those we disciple.

Properly saying that something is against Scripture is not judgmental. This comes out of a love for truth and a desire to live according to the ways of our King. Correctly using the Word of Truth is a call on our lives, and if seen as a negative, will be a huge obstacle for the body of Christ.

For example, I am privileged to mentor many young adults, but I also know it comes with great responsibility. Someone had asked me at one point why God tells us to avoid psychics. My spirit said that they are dangerous and they are a vessel from the pit, but how can I back that up? I began to pray for more revelation about this.

I prayed off and on for months and studied Scripture. I learned that the Bible warns us to avoid psychics many times in Scripture. But even though I knew the Bible states to avoid them, I asked the Lord to take me even deeper.

My answer finally came when my husband and I went to New Orleans on a business trip. One of the evening events included psychics, mystics, and palm readers that were hired for the evening. Little did I know that the next day God would use the evening to answer my questions.

I was sitting at a golf event the following afternoon in front of two ladies that were talking about the prior evening. They both stated that they were completely unraveled, and neither had slept since visiting the psychic. My ears perked up. One lady said she was still struggling to concentrate and had no appetite.

I then turned in my chair and apologized for eavesdropping, but wanted to hear what happened. They both explained that the psychic was amazing, knowing personal information about each of them and their families. But for both of them, the psychic got a concerned look on her face and pronounced that she saw tragedy coming to their families. For one family this mystic said she saw a terrible car accident coming in their future with a loss of something that she holds dear. Coincidently, this woman's daughter was just getting her license. She was visibly shaking just talking about it.

I looked at them and said, "Stop right there. First, Satan knows your past and that is how this psychic could glean some credibility. But he does not know the future, and his only goal was to instill fear in you and rob your joy in Christ." (It makes me laugh now, because at the time I did not even know if they believed in Jesus.) These dear ladies cried with relief when I told them that. I went on to explain what I had learned regarding psychics from Scripture. It was clearly a divine appointment and so powerful because not only did I receive my answer, but God used me to bring truth to these women who were so paralyzed by fear.

Contacting a psychic is not only an affront to God when we should be going to Him for any worry about the future, but it is also a tool Satan uses to rock our faith. He loves to rob our joy in Christ, replace it with fear, and immobilize us. You can call me judgmental when I warn someone against these things, but using the Word of God to distinguish His path for myself or someone else is not being judgmental. I am not saying that seeing a psychic is going to send someone to hell; I am saying that going to a psychic is not good for you and will not benefit your Christian walk. I would still love my neighbor if they were a psychic, knowing that they are deceived and believing that if they see Jesus and His love for them in me, they will eventually be attracted to His story.

We all can struggle at times with assessing someone else's actions as unchristian and point fingers. But God wants us to focus on judging our own actions. Only God knows a person's heart and their story. He is the judge. Point someone to Jesus by living a life of love and they will find what we have found; a God they want to serve and an example in Christ to live up to. One of the greatest deterrents from God is a judging Christian. We misrepresent God every time we stand up in hate and self-righteousness and serve Satan instead.

Our goal as ambassadors is to make Jesus known. We can represent Him well through love, but sometimes we will actually have to talk about Him. This can be a hard thing to do. The name *Jesus* can be controversial, and at times we feel the tension. It is naturally tough at first to bring up His name with people who don't follow Him, but this can even prove hard between believers. If someone loves the Word and quotes the Bible, they can be seen as judgmental. So often those that have been judged will prejudge others. We often become what we hate.

It is ridiculous to end up in this cat-and-mouse routine, trying to bring God glory without being judged by the Christians around us. We can't afford for this to get worse. Let's love one another like crazy and give people the grace that God gives us. We can accept that we are not going to see every detail of life the same, but we all love Jesus, and we are all growing to be more like Him. Not everything that has been revealed to one person has been revealed to others. Unless we think we deserve grace, we shouldn't be afraid to give it to others.

> **Unless we think we deserve grace, we shouldn't be afraid to give it to others.**

At the time that I was writing this chapter, there was an incident where eighty-eight Christians were kidnapped by militants and were facing torture and death. I have a feeling that these Christians were standing united and not arguing about the hot topics of our day. I love Paul's words about love in Corinthians.

> "For the *love* of Christ *controls* us, having concluded this, that one died for all, therefore all died; and He died for all, so that they who live might no longer live for themselves, but for Him who died and rose again on their behalf" (2 Corinthians 5:14-15 emphasis mine).

Paul and his friends tried to make every choice out of honor to God. They allowed His way to be their guide and worked with purpose. The word *control* is so audacious, and it is no surprise that letting love control their actions caused them to move mountains for the kingdom. The Message version describes this so well in the next verse (2 Corinthians 5:16). Paul says that going on from a place of love they don't look at people and judge them, because "They did that to the Messiah and got that wrong already." They strive instead to look at the inside of people and see what God sees. These next verses are so inspiring.

> "God put the world square with Himself through the Messiah, giving the world a fresh start by offering

115

forgiveness of sins. God has given us the task of telling everyone what He is doing. We're Christ's representatives. God uses us to persuade men and women to drop their differences and enter into God's work of making things right between them. We're speaking for Christ himself now: Become friends with God; He's already a friend with you" (2 Corinthians 5:18-20 MSG).

Satan would rather have us treat people poorly, casting a dark shadow on the body of Christ. He will always be pushing us to be prideful and judgmental. But since we are aligning ourselves with Christ, let's represent Him well.

> "Therefore, we are ambassadors for Christ, *as though God were making an appeal through us*" (2 Corinthians 5:20a, emphasis mine).

We had to come full circle and remember that God deserves good representation. When we misrepresent God it can cause people to lose interest in pursuing Him. Thankfully, when God sees us through Christ He is not focusing on our sins. So let's see each other through that lens too. Instead of seeing our differences, let's enjoy our common goal. I have been mentoring people long enough to see the long-term consequences of a child of God feeling shoved out of God's family. It is a chasm that takes a miracle to fill once a believer misrepresents Christ and shames another Christian. It becomes a sensitive situation and takes a precise prayerful effort to even get the privilege to continue sharing in their lives. They end up a saved believer who does not want to be involved with the body of Christ, but loves Jesus. We have so many people in the body who are crying out for healing. Let's stop the bleeding.

We will all become disenchanted with a church or have some Christian we admire let us down at some point, and it is very difficult not to lose interest in the Jesus they represent. But if we have been misrepresented, isn't it possible that Jesus has been too?

TIME FOR THE WARRIOR POSE—THE FIERCENESS OF LOVE

We need to measure our words, seek counsel, and be slow to speak. The body of Christ works best when it is filled to the brim with people with different gifts. At our core, we will never be the same, so let's quit striving for sameness and celebrate the beauty of the unique body of Jesus. Thinking about this responsibility can make us so grateful for God's grace. Today we can try a little harder. He has never expected perfection, but progress.

At our core, we will never be the same, so let's quit striving for sameness and celebrate the beauty of the unique body of Jesus.

The time to testify is now. Let's begin to move forward as one body again. After all the training we have done together in this book, we are now the Special Forces team in God's army.

We are warriors of salt and light that can transform any room we enter. We will choose love fiercely and bring God's perspective to the challenges set before us. We will train in His Word along our comrades, so that even when we are alone we are strong for battle. Our commander will occasionally give us a battle plan that requires the prayers of others, and often we will pray for those out on assignment. We will be a voice for the orphans, the widows, the hungry, and the lost in this world. We will protect the helpless with all our might, and serve people otherwise ignored by society.

We may sometimes be a sniper who brings truth to someone's life, taking out the enemies plan, but most of the time we can be found at our Lanista's feet, gaining His perspective regarding our next move. We will be known as followers of the wisest King, and will bear a likeness to His ways despite the trouble it brings in this life, knowing that we already walk in eternity and this is not our home.

We will be close to the battle field no matter what we are doing until the rapture comes or we are called home. This war is not over. Sometimes we will be wounded, sometimes we will need rest, but in Christ we will keep gaining victories for ourselves and others.

THE TIME TO TESTIFY

When we battle now, we have the spiritual muscle and power in Christ to bring to the fight. When we picture the Colosseum, we are no longer filled with fear, but we can see our adversary pinned to the ground with our foot placed firmly over his throat. For now, we are not going to hear his deceptive words. His thugs are silenced also when they see their leader wanting to flee.

Now we can turn our ears completely to the heavens, gain clarity, and feel the fullness of God's love washing over us. The silence of the arena is palpable as the crowd is perplexed that although we are small, we took out a large adversary, and they have lost their bet. But at this point, we raise our arms to heaven, bring glory to God, and let out our best victory cry. For we know that Jesus once again came to our rescue, and brought His strength and miracles to our plight. The Holy Spirit in us rejoices that hell has been defeated, and Satan's plans for us have been foiled.

In our last gesture before the crowd, we bow our knees to the Most High King, and enjoy the peace that comes to one who is strong in Christ, built up in the Word, and ready to love through another battle.

Eventually we will arrive, still full of sand, before our Father in heaven. Our battle will be over, but the cries of the crowd will be fresh in our memories. At this point, our Lanista will pull us in an embrace and whisper, "Well done. Your battle is over, come taste and see, all that I have purchased just for you." From here, the victory celebration will never end and we will finally leave the war zone behind. May it be friends, may it be!

Meet Jessie Hermann
Junior at Hope College
Holland Michigan

Midway through my sophomore year in college the Lord gave me an idea. I was reading through 1 Corinthians and I kept coming back to chapter 13. I didn't know what the Lord wanted to show me about it, until

118

one day when I was reading it again and I heard the word *identity*. As I read those verses over and over again, the Lord spoke to me. In 1 John 4, we are told that God is love. I saw the picture of Christ taking my place on the cross, of Jesus setting me free by His blood and giving me a new identity as a child of the Most High. I read these verses over and over to myself with the picture of Jesus in mind, but replacing the word *love* with *Jesus*. "*Jesus* is patient, *Jesus* is kind. *Jesus* does not envy, *Jesus* does not boast, *Jesus* is not proud. *Jesus* does not dishonor others, *Jesus* is not self-seeking, *Jesus* is not easily angered, *Jesus* keeps no record of wrongs. *Jesus* does not delight in evil but rejoices with the truth. *Jesus* always protects, always trusts, always hopes, always perseveres." As I read these words the Lord whispered *identity* to me. Then I realized what it truly means to live in the power of the resurrection and to have Jesus living inside of me. Jesus calls us "co-heirs" with Him, and He calls us to be love wherever we are—love is our identity. Since we are called to the standard of love that Jesus displayed on the cross, we can also insert our names for *love*. I would declare these verses over my life every day, and I started to see how the Lord saw me: "*Jessie* is patient, *Jessie* is kind. *Jessie* does not envy, *Jessie* does not boast, *Jessie* is not proud. *Jessie* does not dishonor others, Jessie is not self-seeking, *Jessie* is not easily angered, *Jessie* keeps no record of wrongs. *Jessie* does not delight in evil but rejoices with the truth. *Jessie* always protects, always trusts, always hopes, always perseveres."

Meet Allison Fries
Freshman at University of Wisconsin Eau Claire
Eau Claire, Wisconsin

Love conquers all. Love gets us through the impossible situations that don't look possible to break through. When I went to camp before my freshman year in high school, I gave my life to Jesus. When I came home from camp, my parents told me they were getting a divorce. As a new believer who had dedicated her life to Jesus, all I could hold onto was the truth that He loved me and that His love would bring me through this season of my life. That love has carried me through every day since then.

It carries me through the good and the bad of life. His love conquers all. Why is love the most powerful thing on this earth? Because God is love, as seen in 1 John 4. We serve the God of the impossible. God can conquer anything and everything, and He dominates with love.

Chapter 10: Revival in Rome

"Some died by stoning, some were sawed in half, and others were killed with the sword. Some went about wearing skins of sheep and goats, destitute and oppressed and mistreated. They were too good for this world, wandering over deserts and mountains, hiding in caves and holes in the ground. All these people earned a good reputation because of their faith, yet none of them received all that God had promised. For God had something better in mind for us, so that they would not reach perfection without us" (Hebrews 11:37-40 NLT).

The Colosseum today bears a cross on its grounds in honor of the many Christian martyrs that lost their lives in the most gruesome of ways.

Jesus went on trial under a governor of Rome, Pontius Pilate, when he was sentenced to His death (Luke 23). The emperor of Rome at the time was Tiberius. Pontius Pilate did not believe Jesus was guilty of any crimes, but he was in a political bind when he handed down the decision to place Him on the cross.

Jesus defeated death, and rose again to appear to His followers. Shortly after, He returned to His Father in heaven. The time was perfect for the Holy Spirit to come, as there were Christians from all over the world gathered together, waiting and praying for direction. The Holy Spirit filled them all and these Christians instantly became victors instead of victims, just like us (Acts 4).

This Holy Spirit is the same power that raised Jesus from the dead, and it was now leading them home to their battlegrounds. I can picture them all caravanning and rejoicing for miles as they left Jerusalem for home. In unity, they prayed and believed that revival could come to their nations. They returned home and began a life of sacrificial love that carries on to this day. We are the result of their legacy. We are still receiving the blessings from their battles.

Rome received some of these Christians, and even the apostle Paul came and stayed a few years around 65 A.D. Paul was technically under house arrest during this time period, and was eventually beheaded under the leadership of Nero. Nero was one of the most ruthless Emperors to reign over Rome. During his reign the majority of Rome was burned in 64 A.D. in a ruthless fire. It is rumored that Nero started the fire, and shortly after he added on to his own humongous palace over the freshly charred land.

It is recorded that Nero diverted the blame for the fire on the Christians at the time, and he sentenced several hundred of them to death. It is believed that the disciple Peter was one of those martyred. Peter was crucified upside down because he did not feel worthy to die the same death of Jesus, his Master and Friend. Whether Peter was in this original group is up for debate, but it is certain that these Christians were ruthlessly murdered.

Some were killed by animals for the amusement of a crowd, some had their skin boiled and then had to sit in salt and vinegar, and many were burned at the stake to light up the night sky. Nero felt the fire from the stakes would help the citizens celebrate the Christian's fate late into the evening. According to some reports, many of the Roman citizens started to feel bad for the Christians. One is willing to bet that there were many undiscovered Christians who were forced to celebrate this horrible event.

The apostle Paul died during Nero's reign shortly after the large Christian massacre. Paul was beheaded because he was a Roman citizen and legally could not be hung on the cross.

Interestingly, Rome had several leaders after Nero that worshipped many other gods. It was not until Emperor Constantine rose to power, who reigned almost three hundred years after Christ's death, that Rome became a Christian Empire. Many Christians were martyred on the sand of the Colosseum between Nero and Constantine, and this should give us pause.

I believe that the purest battle between darkness and light is one the crowd notices. When these slaves and gladiators were put to the test, God's glory shined through. When darkness tries to shut out the light, the light only gets more blinding. By God's grace, between Nero and Constantine the numbers of Christians in Rome climbed. There is no putting out a fire that God starts. We can be sure that Nero did not realize the fire he started was also spiritual, and that God would use his evil plans for good.

> **The purest battle between darkness and light is one the crowd notices.**

Being a Christian was not an easy road in these days, but because of their fight, we are blessed. If they ran from the battle, where would we be today?

They remind us that our peace in battle is being recognized by the people around us. When we walk by faith and live in obedience, the crowd around us pays attention; not because we are so special, but because Jesus is. He lives in us and gives us strength from a well that never runs dry.

Revival Happens because of the Battle

Metaphorically, because of Jesus, as we step onto the sandy floor, we stand firm. We are being carried by the prayer of other warriors, and whether we are there to defend ourselves or a comrade, we are nearly unshakable. Our confident gaze and set shoulders as we take in the scene will give our enemy reason for pause. Suddenly, the confidence he had when he was warming up the crowd begins to slip, and it is beginning to show on his face. He thought this would be easy, but even though they outnumber us today, he senses that his weak thugs won't last the first round. This crowd has seen us battle before, and they know to place their bets in our favor. Secretly, they are beginning to cheer for the Christians.

Like experienced fighters, we predict the moves of the enemy and quickly take them down. With ease, Satan's plan is thwarted, and he and his minions slink away to lick their wounds. A few of us are injured in this fight but will be easily tended by our comrades.

The crowd sees the cost of our commitment to Christ, and although they won't publicly applaud us, they are tempted to hear more.

The crowd sees the cost of our commitment to Christ, and although they won't publicly applaud us, they are tempted to hear more. For now, they know who to ask if they find themselves brave enough to go against the mainstream. As we pray for them, and unite in battle, our numbers eventually grow. Eventually our battleground will see revival, and the crowd will rise in worship to the one True King.

Today, Rome is still a Christian city, and if Rome could experience revival, so can America. What blessings do we want to bring the generations that follow us? Our battle will affect them for better or worse. Let's link arms and listen to our lanista. Until we meet in battle—or in heaven—I am grateful we are on the same team. Carry on, friends, and to God be the glory!

Notes

Information regarding the Colosseum and its Gladiators has been retrieved from two websites:

"Gladiators." *Gladiators*. N.p., n.d. Web. 13 Nov. 2015. <http://www.tribunesandtriumphs.org/gladiators>.

History.com Staff."Colosseum." *History.com*. A&E Television Networks, 2009. Web. 10 Oct. 2015. <http://www.history.com/topics/ancient-history/colosseum>.

Chapter 1
"National Center for Education Statistics (NCES) Home Page, a Part of the U.S. Department of Education." *National Center for Education Statistics (NCES) Home Page, a Part of the U.S. Department of Education.* N.p., Apr. 2014. Web. 13 Nov. 2015. <https://nces.ed.gov/> – graduation facts.

Montana Camp – Lions Ridge Adventure Camp www.lionsridge.com.

Chapter 2
Information for the last American Revival was gleaned from the following websites:

"Jesus Movement." *Wikipedia*. Wikimedia Foundation, 9 Sept. 2015. Web. 22 Sept. 2015. <https://en.wikipedia.org/wiki/Jesus_movement>.

Baxter, Addie. "Hippies Were Outspoken, Anti-war Activists and Anything but Slackers." N.p., 5 Jan. 2010. Web. 20 Sept. 2015. <http://www2.readingeagle.com/article.aspx?id=183468>.

History.com Staff. "Vietnam War Protests." *History.com*. A&E Television Networks, 2010. Web. 20 Sept. 2015. <http://www.history.com/topics/vietnam-war/vietnam-war-protests>.

Brownsville Revival. (2015, July). Retrieved February 16, 2016, from https://en.wikipedia.org/wiki/Brownsville_Revival.

Chapter 3
Colisseum and Gladiators – Triumphs and Tribunes, History.com as stated above.

Chapter 5
Herb Brooks story was included with permission from his family and foundation.

"About Coach Brooks." *Herb Brooks Foundation*. N.p., n.d. Web. 8 Mar. 2015. <http://www.herbbrooksfoundation.com/page/show/701796-about-coach-brooks>.

"Herb Brooks Speech - Heros and the History of Sports." *Herb Brooks Speech - Heros and the History of Sports*. N.p., n.d. Web. 13 Oct. 2014. <https://sites.google.com/site/herosandthehistoryofsports/herb-brooks-speech>.

"1980 U.S. Olympic Team." *U.S. Hockey Hall of Fame*. U.S. Hockey, n.d. Web. 13 Nov. 2015. <http://www.ushockeyhalloffame.com/page/show/831562-the-1980-u-s-olympic-team>.

"Presidency of Jimmy Carter." *Wikipedia*. Wikimedia Foundation, n.d. Web. 1 Nov. 2014. <https://en.wikipedia.org/wiki/Presidency_of_Jimmy_Carter>.

Chapter 6

Lewis, C.S. Mere Christianity. New York: Macmillan, 1960.

Chapter 7

Stuart, Ben. *"The Lord's Prayer."* StudentLife. Alabama. June 2013. Lecture.

Taylor, Paul S. "Christian Answers Network, The Truth about Angelic Beings." *Christian Answers Network [Home] • Multilingual Answers, Reviews, Ministry Resources, and More! • ChristianAnswers.Net*. Films for Christ, n.d. Web. 1 Oct. 2015. <http://www.christiananswers.net/>.

Chapter 9

Birthing Center:

"Action International Ministries, Shalom Birthing Center." *Action International*. N.p., n.d. Web. 13 Nov. 2015. <https://www.actioninternational.org/>.

Fritz, Nancy. "The Fritz Farm." *The Fritz Farm*. N.p., n.d. Web. Aug. 2014. <http://r7thheaven.blogspot.com/>.

About the Author

Barb lives in Plymouth, Minnesota with her husband of twenty-five years, Mark, and her six children. At this point, her seventeen-year-old son, Bradley, and her sixteen-year-old daughter, Abby—the artist for this cover, are still at home. Barb is currently finishing her bachelors in Christian ministries at Bethel University. She is also currently a staff member at Bethel University and a youth leader at a ministry called The Basement. Barb has a real passion for making Jesus known and loves to spend time with family, exercise with friends, and study the Word with people who long to know more about Jesus. Nothing makes her day like a call from her kids or a fresh word from her King.

For more information about Barb, visit:
www.barbyo.com.

CPSIA information can be obtained
at www.ICGtesting.com
Printed in the USA
FFOW05n0542210616

9 781942 056263